AIRLINE LIVERIES

Third Edition
Günter Endres

IAN ALLAN
Publishing

Introduction

There have always been functional elements to the painting of aircraft, though these are perhaps of lesser importance today than in the very early days when a coat of paint on wood- and fabric-covered aircraft provided some modicum of protection from inclement weather. Heat generation rather than weather on modern high-speed and high-flying aircraft is a problem minimised by light-coloured or white upper fuselage, which reflect the rays of the sun. By contrast, aircraft bellies which get particularly dirty are usually of grey or darker shades.

The clean shapes of modern jet aircraft have inspired more visually pleasing and highly visible designs, with bands of co-ordinated colour 'cheatlines' sweeping along the fuselage and up the tailfin, and in some particularly attractive instances, wrapped around the aircraft. Stylised bird symbols still predominate on the less imaginative designs. Colours used often reflect those of the national flag, or allude to the airline's purpose. In the latter instance, for example, holiday charter airlines generally favour orange, yellow and blue to represent sun, sand and sky.

Occasionally, airlines have one or two aircraft painted in a completely different scheme to highlight a special event or theme, the All Nippon Airways 'Snoopy' cartoon character, the Qantas 'Wunala Dreaming' Aborigine painting, and the Austrian Airlines 'millenium' A321, being recent examples. Product advertising, especially in the United States, is beginning to transform aircraft into giant billboards which,

while colourful, is an unwelcome trend. Leasing aircraft for short periods to overcome temporary shortages has proliferated over recent times, giving rise to numerous short-term hybrid schemes. These often reflect a mix of markings of the airline providing the aircraft and those of the interim operator, with the latter sometimes only applying its titles.

But instant recognition of all facets of an airline's operation is today's name of the game. The 'total concept', that is full co-ordination of aircraft paint scheme, vehicles, stationery, shops, check-in desks, staff uniforms and thousands of smaller items, is now being implemented by virtually every carrier throughout the industry. There is no doubt that the modern transport aircraft has been turned into the most visible flying advertising hoarding; one that appears repeatedly on the numerous regular destinations of the airline's route network, in the case of major airlines, all over the world.

Günter Endres
Lindfield

Cover and title page:
A variety of liveries seen at London Gatwick. *Nick Hall*

All photographs via the Author unless otherwise credited.

First published 1991
Second Edition 1995
Third Edition 1997

ISBN 0 7110 2519 3

© Ian Allan Ltd 1997

Published by Ian Allan Publishing

an imprint of Ian Allan Ltd, Terminal House, Station Approach, Shepperton, Surrey TW17 8AS.
Printed by Ian Allan Printing Ltd at its works at Coombelands in Runnymede, England.

Code: 9706/E

FLEET #S

Contents

ADRIA AIRWAYS (JP/ADR)

Founded/First Service: 1961
Base: Brnik Airport, Ljubljana, Slovenia
Services: International scheduled services from Ljubljana to Amsterdam, Barcelona, Copenhagen, Frankfurt, Glasgow, London Heathrow, Manchester (summer only), Moscow, Munich, Paris (jointly with Air France), Prague (with Czech Airlines), Tel Aviv, Tirana, Vienna and Zürich. Also a domestic network serving Skopje, Split and Ljubljana, together with air taxi services linking 25 towns and cities in Slovenia. Charter flights to destinations in Europe and Africa, particularly to Antalya and Istanbul in Turkey, Tunis in Tunisia and Las Palmas in the Canary Islands.
Fleet (7): 3 x Airbus A320-200, 2 x Douglas DC-9-32,
2 x de Havilland Canada DHC-7-100.
Adria Aviotaxi: 1 x Cessna 441 Conquest, 1 x Piper PA-34-220T Seneca III.
Colour scheme: Large and bold 'ADRIA' titles in blue take up half of the clean all-white fuselage, being highly visible from a distance. The airline's insignia, which depicts the first letter 'A' in blue reflected in the turquoise waters of the Adriatic, dominates the tailfin. On the Airbus A320, the insignia is repeated on the engine cowlings.
Illustrated: The Adria Airways fleet is headed by the Airbus A320, which first entered service with the airline in May 1989 and is pictured here on a frosty morning at Ljubljana/Brnik. Two more were acquired in September the following year.

AER LINGUS (EI/EIN)

Founded/First Service: 22 May 1936
Base: Dublin Airport, Dublin, Eire
Services: European routes from the Irish Republic to Amsterdam, Birmingham, Bristol, Brussels, Copenhagen, Düsseldorf, Edinburgh, Frankfurt, Glasgow, Hamburg, Jersey, Leeds Bradford, London, Madrid, Manchester, Milan, Newcastle, Paris, Rennes, Rome, Stuttgart and Zürich. Transatlantic services from Dublin and Shannon to Boston, Chicago and New York/JFK and Newark, and from Belfast to New York. Domestic system includes Dublin, Cork, Galway, Kerry County, Knock, Shannon and Sligo.
Fleet (28): 4 x Airbus A330-300, 2 x 737-400, 10 x 737-500, 6 x BAe 146-300, 6 x Fokker 50.
Colour scheme: The new corporate identity was launched on 14 February 1996 with a concept developed by Luxon Carra, designed to capture the essence of Aer Lingus: Irish, vibrant, dynamic, responsive, natural and 'green'. It features a reworked shamrock on the tail with more fluid and natural lines, and softer colours of three shades of green, a petrol blue and a grey, covering the upper part of the crisp white fuselage, said to evoke a lush and verdant landscape, interspersed with clean lakes and rivers and overcast with mist-laden skies. The name is applied forward in a flowing typography, resembling the written word and reminiscent of a new literary theme embodied in excerpts from the writings of Irish poets, novelists and playwrights, reproduced on many airline items.
Illustrated: Aer Lingus became the first operator of the Airbus A330 across the Atlantic in May 1994, linking Dublin and Shannon with New York and Boston.

AEROFLOT RUSSIAN INTERNATIONAL AIRLINES (SU/AFL)

Founded/First Service: 9 February 1923 as Dobrolet/Aeroflot name adopted 1932
Base: Sheremetyevo Airport, Moscow, Russian Federation
Services: Extensive international flights to 135 destinations in Europe, Africa, Middle East, Far East and North, Central and South America. All important cities in Europe are scheduled and the network extends as far as Tokyo, Jakarta, Anchorage, San Francisco, Santiago de Chile and Johannesburg. Domestic flights are operated by another division, as well as several new affiliated companies based on former Aeroflot directorates.
Fleet (116): 10 x Airbus A310-300, 2 x Boeing 767-200ER, 28 x Ilyushin IL-62M, 14 x IL-76TD, 19 x IL-86, 5 x IL-96-300, 1 x McDonnell Douglas DC-10-30F, 8 x Tupolev Tu-134A-3, 25 x Tu-154M, 4 x Tu-204C.
Colour scheme: Aeroflot's traditional livery which features the Russian flag on a white fuselage, interrupted only by twin blue cheatlines, may be replaced by a new scheme currently carried on the Tupolev Tu-204. This incorporates large Aeroflot titles in Cyrillic followed by the words 'RUSSIAN INTERNATIONAL AIRLINES' in much smaller lettering and preceded by its historic winged hammer and sickle logo, all in blue. Twin blue cheatlines separate the upper white body from the lower metal finish of the aircraft. Six blue and six red bands take up the lower two-thirds of the tailfin.
Illustrated: The Airbus A310-300 was the first Western aircraft to enter the fleet of the new Aeroflot, following the break-up of the Soviet Union. A total of 10 are operated on important long-haul routes.

AEROLINEAS ARGENTINAS (AR/ARG)

Founded/First Service: May 1949
Base: Ezeiza Airport, Buenos Aires, Argentina
Services: Extensive scheduled passenger and cargo services throughout Central and South America; to Miami, New York, Los Angeles, Montreal and Toronto; and across the Atlantic to Amsterdam, Frankfurt, London, Madrid, Paris, Rome and Zürich. Trans-Pacific routes link Buenos Aires to Sydney and Auckland. Domestic trunk services are also flown.
Fleet (36): 3 x Airbus A310-300, 8 x Boeing 727-200, 10 x 737-200C, 6 x 747-200B, 3 x Fokker F28-1000, 6 x McDonnell Douglas MD-88.
Colour scheme: Aerolineas Argentinas' latest livery features twin cheatlines in light and royal blue on an otherwise all-white aircraft, which sweep down from behind the cockpit and along the fuselage at and above window level. The traditional condor insignia in royal blue dominates the white tailfin. 'AEROLINEAS ARGENTINAS' titles are reversed out in white and set into the upper royal blue cheatline ahead of the wing.
Illustrated: Long-haul services between South America and Europe are flown by the Boeing 747-200B, fitted out for 391 passengers in a two-class configuration.

AERO LLOYD (YP/AEF)

Founded/First Service: 6 September 1979/21 March 1980
Base: Frankfurt Rhein/Main Airport, Frankfurt, Germany
Services: Inclusive-tour holiday charters from Berlin, Düsseldorf, Frankfurt and Hamburg to resorts in the Mediterranean Basin and to the Canary Islands. Typical destinations include Adana, Alicante, Almeria, Amman, Antalya, Arrecife, Catania, Chania, Corfu, Faro, Fuerteventura, Heraklion, Hurghada, Ibiza, Kefalonia, Kos, Las Palmas, Lisbon, Luxor, Mahon, Malaga, Marrakech, Monastir, Mykonos, Naples, Olbia, Palma de Mallorca, Rhodes, Santorini, Sharm el Sheikh, Tel Aviv, Thessaloniki and Zakynthos.
Fleet (26): 6 x Airbus A320-200, 2 x McDonnell Douglas MD-82, 14 x MD-83, 4 x MD-87. *On order:* 6 x Airbus A321-100.
Colour scheme: Aero Lloyd's new simpler but effective scheme was introduced with the delivery of the Airbus A320 in early 1996. The clean white fuselage is adorned only with the company's blue and red symbol, a modern transformation of the letters 'A' and 'L' into a speed arrow on the tailfin, repeated on the engine cowlings, and the airline name ahead of the wing below the cabin windows. The blue and red colours also appear on the winglets of the Airbus.
Illustrated: Aero Lloyd placed an order for twin-engined single-aisle Airbuses in 1995, which will eventually replace the McDonnell Douglas MD-80 fleet. The first A320-200 was delivered in January 1996, with the larger A321 to follow from March 1998.

AEROMEXICO (AM/AMX)

Founded/First Service: 15 September 1934 as Aeronaves de Mexico, present name adopted 28 January 1972
Base: Benito Juarez International Airport, Mexico City, Mexico
Services: Vast domestic network to 40 towns and cities, together with scheduled services to the United States and across the Atlantic to Europe. International destinations are Atlanta, Dallas/Ft Worth, Houston, Madrid, Miami, Los Angeles, New Orleans, New York/JFK, Orlando, Paris, Phoenix, San Diego and Tucson. Marketing, code-share or block-space agreement with other airlines extends long-haul system.
Fleet (48): 6 x Boeing 757-200, 2 x 767-300ER,
18 x McDonnell Douglas DC-9-31/32, 10 x MD-82, 2 x MD-87, 10 x MD-88.
Colour scheme: The present livery was introduced following the airline's privatisation in 1988. It retains its famous Mexican birdman motif on a mid-blue tailfin, with the airline name at the base, given a speed emphasis through a blue and white gradation of the word 'Aero'. The blue extends the length of the fuselage in a broad window stripe, accompanied by a lower red cheatline of the same width, the two lines separating the roof from the lower fuselage, both finished in natural metal. The colour scheme reflects the national flag which is carried above the front cabin windows.
Illustrated: The Aeromexico fleet is now headed by Boeing twinjets, including the 757, used primarily on its routes to the United States. *Terry Shone*

AIR 2000 (DP/AMM)

Founded/First Service: 11 April 1987
Bases: Manchester International Airport and London Gatwick, United Kingdom
Services: Intensive charter programmes from Manchester, London Gatwick, Glasgow, Birmingham, Bristol and Newcastle to the principal holiday destinations around the Mediterranean and long-haul flights to North America, the Caribbean, Latin America and the Far East, regularly serving resorts in Antigua, Barbados, Cuba, Dominican Republic, Mexico, USA, Venezuela, Sri Lanka and Thailand. Larnaca and Paphos in Cyprus are served on a scheduled basis from Gatwick and Birmingham.
Fleet (17): 4 x Airbus A320-200, 13 x Boeing 757-200.
Colour scheme: The UK charter airline unveiled a new look for its aircraft on 30 October 1996. Designed by Landor Associates, it combines the distinctive colours of its parent company First Choice with evocative holiday images from around the world through a tapestry of vivid colours and bold shapes. The distinctive 'swoop' shape of the tapestry on the sides is inspired by the aircraft's aerodynamic qualities and adds to its visual momentum, while the unique use of the tapestry's colours on both upper and lower wings takes advantage of a previously unexploited device for communicating identity. Titles are in blue above the forward cabin windows.
Illustrated: The Boeing 757 in the new group colours.

AIR AFRIQUE (RK/RKA)

Founded/First Service: 28 March 1961 as multinational carrier for 11 former French colonies
Base: Port Bouet International Airport, Abidjan, Ivory Coast
Services: Scheduled passenger and cargo services connecting capital cities of member states with each other and with long-haul destinations in Europe, the Middle East and across the Atlantic. Cities served are: Abidjan, Bamako, Bangui, Bissau, Bordeaux, Brazzaville, Conakry, Cotonou, Dakar, Douala, Jeddah, Johannesburg, Lagos, Libreville, Lisbon, Lomé, Lyon, Marseille, N'Djamena, New York/JFK, Niamey, Nouakchott, Ouagadougou, Paris, Pointe Noire and Rome.
Fleet (14): 3 x Airbus A300B4-200, 2 x A300-600R, 6 x A310-300,
2 x Boeing 737-200, 1 x McDonnell Douglas DC-10-30.
Colour scheme: As a multinational carrier, Air Afrique chose neutral bright shades of lime green and emerald green to colour the broad cheatlines, with the lime green along the windows and the emerald below, on the otherwise snow-white aircraft. Centrepiece of the tail is a gazelle's head spanning a globe, both in matching emerald green, symbolising the airline's far-reaching and speedy services. Bold 'AIR AFRIQUE' titles are applied in black on the forward upper fuselage.
Illustrated: Flagship of the fleet is the Airbus
A310-300 twinjet, first delivered in April 1991.

AIR ALGÉRIE (AH/DAH)

Founded/First Service: 1946 as Compagnie Générale de Transports Aériens (CGTA), present name adopted in April 1953 after merger with Compagnie Air Transport (CAT)

Base: Houari Boumedienne Airport, Algiers, Algeria

Services: Scheduled passenger and cargo services to destinations in North and West Africa, Europe and the Middle East. Cities served in Europe include Amsterdam, Athens, Barcelona, Belgrade, Brussels, Bucharest, Frankfurt, Lille, Lyon, London, Madrid, Marseille, Metz, Moscow, Nice, Paris, Prague, Rome, Sofia, Toulouse and Zürich. An extensive domestic network is also operated, together with air taxi and agricultural flying.

Fleet (49): 4 x Airbus A310-200, 3 x Beechcraft 65-B80 Queen Air,
2 x King Air A100, 10 x Boeing 727-200, 16 x 737-200/C, 3 x 767-300,
8 x Fokker F27-400M, 3 x Lockheed L-382G Hercules.

Colour scheme: Introduced in mid-1982, the scheme is built around the national colours of red, green and white and features two thin red stripes separated by a broader green band. The upper red sweeps up and over the rear fuselage into a wide sash. An all-white tail displays the company's red insignia, said to represent its two-letter code 'AH' in the shape of a bird. English and Arabic titles are applied side by side on the upper fuselage.

Illustrated: Air Algérie remains one of a dwindling number of airlines which still uses large numbers of Boeing 727-200s. Its aircraft were delivered over a 10-year period from 1971.

AIR BALTIC (BT/BTI)

Founded/First Service: 23 July 1992 as Baltic International Airlines (BIA), present title adopted 1 October 1995 when merged with Latavio

Base: Riga Spilve Airport, Riga, Latvia

Services: National flag-carrier providing international scheduled passenger and cargo services from Riga to Berlin Schönefeld, Copenhagen, Frankfurt, Hamburg, Helsinki, Kiev, Minsk, Moscow, London Gatwick, St Petersburg, Stockholm, Tallinn, Vilnius and Warsaw. Intends to extend operations to Athens, Budapest, Düsseldorf and Sofia.

Fleet (4): 3 x Avro RJ70, 1 x Saab 340A.

Colour scheme: The colour scheme has been evolving since the airline started operations following independence. This present scheme, first adopted on the Saab 340A, has a clean look, distinguished by an all-white fuselage and a blue and white chequerboard tailfin. 'air Baltic' titles in blue, with the letter 'B' tilted and designed to match the tail application, are painted low on the forward fuselage. The airline title is repeated on the white engine cowlings. The national flag of maroon and white appears alongside the rear door.

Illustrated: Mainline services are now flown by three Avro RJ70s, which replaced two Boeing 727s from spring 1996. They are operated in two-class, five-abreast seating for 70 passengers.

AIR CANADA (AC/ACA)

Founded/First Service: 10 April 1937 as Trans-Canada Airlines/1 September 1937. Present title adopted 1 January 1965

Base: Dorval Airport, Montreal, Quebec, Canada

Services: Passenger and cargo services to the United States and the Caribbean, together with trans-Pacific routes to Seoul, Hong Kong and Osaka, and across the North Atlantic to Europe, Tel Aviv and New Delhi. Destinations in Europe include Brussels, Düsseldorf, Frankfurt, Glasgow, London, Lyon, Manchester, Paris and Zürich. All major domestic points, with feeder services provided by five regional airlines under the 'Air Canada Connector' network. They are: AirBC, NWT Air, Air Ontario, Air Alliance and Air Nova.

Fleet (138): 5 x Airbus A319, 34 x A320-200, 2 x A340-300, 3 x 747-100, 3 x 747-200, 3 x 747-400, 23 x 767-200, 6 x 767-300ER, 24 x Canadair CL-65 Regional Jet, 35 x McDonnell Douglas DC9-32.

On order: 30 x Airbus A319, 6 x A320-200, 4 x A340-300.

Colour scheme: Prominent red 'AIR CANADA' titles on a simple white body are preceded by the familiar, yet more natural looking, rondel. A huge natural red maple leaf against an evergreen background symbolises the land, its people, its strength and its airline. Unveiled on 1 December 1993, the new identity was created by New York-based consultants, Diefenbach Elkins, to reflect Air Canada's evolution from a Crown Corporation to a fully privatised carrier, while retaining its attributes of tradition, stability and reliability.

Illustrated: Air Canada is taking delivery of six Airbus A340-300s, fitted out with 284 seats in a two-class layout.

AIR CHINA (CA/CCA)

Founded/First Service: 2 November 1949
Base: Capital Airport, Beijing, People's Republic of China
Services: International services from Beijing to Bangkok, Berlin, Copenhagen, Frankfurt, Fukuoka, Helsinki, Jakarta, Karachi, Kuwait, London, Melbourne, Milan, Moscow, New York, Osaka, Paris, Rome, San Francisco, Sendai, Seoul, Singapore, Stockholm, Sydney, Tokyo, Ulan Bator, Vancouver, Vienna, Yangon and Zürich. Apart from Beijing, other Chinese cities linked into the international network are Dalian, Guangzhou, Kunming, Shanghai and Xiamen. Also extensive domestic trunk network.
Fleet (59): 2 x Antonov An-12, 19 x Boeing 737-300, 3 x 747-200B(SCD), 1 x 747-200F, 8 x 747-400, 4 x 747SP, 6 x 767-200(ER), 4 x 767-300, 4 x BAe 146-100, 2 x Lockheed L-100 Hercules, 6 x Xian Y7.
On order: 3 x A340-300.
Colour scheme: A white upper fuselage and grey underside are separated by twin mid-blue cheatlines of different width. Black 'AIR CHINA' titles in English and Chinese characters are preceded by the red national flag incorporating the five-pointed yellow stars. A red phoenix, said by the Chinese to bring good fortune, flies on the white tail. It is cleverly stylised to read 'VIP', illustrating the airline's commitment to service. On the Boeing 747-400, the phoenix is repeated on the winglets.
Illustrated: Flagship of the Air China fleet is the Boeing 747-400, which is replacing the smaller 747SP on its routes to Europe.

AIR FRANCE (AF/AFR)

Founded/First Service: 30 August 1933

Bases: Paris Charles de Gaulle Airport, Roissy and Paris Orly, France

Services: Scheduled passenger and cargo services worldwide, linking France with 165 towns and cities on all continents. Extensive route network within Europe serves 56 destinations plus another eight in metropolitan France. Air France Europe, until 1 January 1996 known as Air Inter, concentrates on domestic services to 31 destinations, while subsidiary Air Charter undertakes short/medium-haul charters.

Fleet (201): 6 x A300B2-100, 5 x Airbus A300B4-200, 5 x A310-200, 4 x A310-300, 5 x A319, 13 x A320-100, 45 x A320-200, 5 x A321-100, 4 x A330-300, 5 x A340-200, 6 x A340-300, 5 x Concorde 100, 17 x Boeing 737-200A, 6 x 737-300, 17 x 737-500, 7 x 747-100, 4 x 747-200B, 6 x 747-200B(SCD), 11 x 747-200F, 2 x 747-300, 7 x 747-400, 6 x 747-400(SCD), 5 x 767-300, 5 x Fokker 100. *On order:* 5 x Airbus A340-300, 10 x Boeing 777-200IGW.

Colour scheme: Based on the French Tricolour, the pure white overall fuselage finish is highlighted by bold blue 'AIR FRANCE' titles forward of the wing, led by its long-established winged seahorse symbol in blue and red. The aircraft's major design element is a splash of colour in the form of blue and red stripes in varying widths sweeping up the tailfin. The colour scheme was introduced in 1975. The Air France Europe scheme is similar with the exception of the title.

Illustrated: Air France became only the second airline (after Lufthansa) to put the Airbus A340-300 into service in March 1993. The A340 is the longest-range airliner in service.

AIR GABON (GN/AGN)

Founded/First Service: 1951 as Compagnie Aérienne Gabonaise, later Société Nationale Transgabon, adopted present title 1974

Base: Leon M'Ba International Airport, Libreville, Gabon

Services: International flag services to London, Marseille, Nice, Paris and Rome, and regionally to Abidjan, Bamako, Bangui, Cotonou, Dakar, Douala, Johannesburg, Lomé, Malabo, Kinshasa, Pointe Noire, Lagos, Sao Tomé and Luanda. Domestic network to 23 points, including the main towns of Port Gentil, Lambarene, Latourville, Makokou, Masuku, Mayumba, Mitzic, Ndjole and Tchibanga.

Fleet (5): 1 x Boeing 737-200A, 1 x 747-200B(SCD), 2 x Fokker F28-2000, 1 x Fokker 100.

Colour scheme: The pure white finish of the aircraft fuselage is further freshened by the airline's stylised green parrot symbol on the tailfin and 'AIR GABON' titles in blue on the forward cabin roof. A patriotic tricolour cheatline in the colours of the national flag runs below the windows and extends the length of the fuselage, cut off at an angle at both ends. The colour green stands for the Gabonese forests, yellow for the warm sun and blue for the abundant sea.

Illustrated: Air Gabon operates its single Boeing 747-200B Combi on all long-haul services, fitted out for 250 passengers in a three-class layout, with additional capacity for 30 tonnes of freight.

AIR INDIA (AI/AIC)

Founded/First Service: 8 March 1948/8 June 1948
Base: Bombay (Mumbai) Airport, Bombay (Mumbai), India
Services: International flag services from Bombay, Delhi, Calcutta, Trivandrum and Madras to Abu Dhabi, Bahrain, Bangkok, Dar es Salaam, Dhahran, Doha, Dubai, Durban, Frankfurt, Geneva, Hong Kong, Jakarta, Jeddah, Johannesburg, Kuala Lumpur, Kuwait, London, Moscow, Muscat, Nairobi, New York, Osaka, Paris, Perth, Rome, Riyadh, Singapore, Tokyo and Toronto.
Fleet (30): 3 x Airbus A300B4-200, 8 x A310-300,
2 x Boeing 747-300(SCD), 9 x 747-200B, 6 x 747-400,
2 x Lockheed L1011 TriStar 500.
Colour scheme: Air India has replaced its golden sun in a deep red ambassadorial sash and has reverted to the scheme designed by the Art Studio of Bombay in conjunction with its own art department and first introduced with the Boeing 747 in May 1971. Each window has a unique temple-style outline framed by a full-length cheatline top and bottom, all in red. A sweeping fin flash, also in red, is superimposed by 'AIR-INDIA' titles. The airline name is repeated in large Hindi script on the upper fuselage, preceded by the national flag.
Illustrated: Air India uses the Airbus A310-300, first delivered in April 1986, on high-density regional services.

AIR JAMAICA (JM/AJM)

Founded/First Service: 1968/1 April 1969
Base: Norman Manley International Airport, Kingston, Jamaica
Services: Privatised national airline providing regional and international passenger services from Kingston and Montego Bay to Atlanta, Baltimore/Washington, Chicago, Ft Lauderdale, Los Angeles, Miami, New York/JFK and Newark, Orlando and Philadelphia in the USA; Grand Cayman and Nassau in the Caribbean; and across the Atlantic to London. Services to the Eastern Caribbean, including Antigua, Barbados and St Lucia, planned for Spring 1997. Domestic feeder services by subsidiary Air Jamaica Express.
Fleet (12): 6 x Airbus A310-300, 4 x A320-200, 2 x Boeing 727-200 Advanced.
Colour scheme: The 'Jamaican flair' colours were introduced following the airline's privatisation in November 1994, as a clear message that it is a new, professional company facing the future with confidence. The splash of bright Caribbean colours, taking up most of the aircraft surface, graduate in varying size bands from golden yellow to orange, magenta and deep purple, ending in a sweep at the rear, with the deep purple covering the tailfin, itself interspersed with magenta and lighter blue stripes. Dominating the tail is Air Jamaica's traditional stylised symbol of a yellow doctor bird, a native of Jamaica. 'air Jamaica' titles in magenta and purple sit atop the orange band on the forward cabin roof.
Illustrated: The Airbus A320-200 forms part of a complete fleet renewal, which also includes the larger A310-300 model.

AIRLANKA (UL/ALK)

Founded/First Service: 10 January 1979/1 September 1979
Base: Bandaranayake International Airport, Colombo, Sri Lanka
Services: International scheduled passenger and cargo services from Colombo eastwards to Bangkok, Hong Kong, Kuala Lumpur, Singapore, Fukuoka and Tokyo, and to Trivandrum, Madras, Tiruchirapally, Bombay, Delhi, Karachi, Male, Abu Dhabi, Bahrain, Dubai, Dhahran, Jeddah, Kuwait, Muscat, Riyadh, Amsterdam, Frankfurt, London, Paris, Rome, Vienna and Zürich.
Fleet (9): 2 x Airbus A320-200, 3 x A340-300,
2 x Lockheed L1011 Tristar 100/50, 2 x L1011 TriStar 500.
Colour scheme: A bright red windowline runs from the nose and spreads out over the entire rear fuselage and tailfin, which forms the backdrop to a large white stylised peacock motif. A thinner red cheatline accompanies the windowline along the whole length. The fuselage is finished in white, with black 'AIRLANKA' titles in capital letters forward of the wing. The Sri Lankan national flag, based on the Sinhalese flag and incorporating a golden lion with sword, framed by four Buddhist pipul leaves, and green and orange stripes to represent Hindu and Muslim minorities, is applied ahead of the titles.
Illustrated: The four-engined Airbus A340-300 is the latest long-haul type to join the AirLanka fleet. The first was delivered in August 1994, followed by another in November and the third in February 1995.

AIR LITTORAL (FU/LIT)

Founded/First Service: April 1972/23 May 1972

Base: Montpellier-Méditerranée Airport, Mauguio, France

Services: Growing domestic and cross-border routes, both on its own behalf and under subcontract to the Air France Group. Points on the route system are Agen, Ajaccio, Avignon, Barcelona, Bergerac, Béziers, Biarritz, Bologna, Bordeaux, Clermont-Ferrand, Düsseldorf, Epinal, Florence, Frankfurt, Geneva, Lille, London, Lourdes/Tarbes, Lyon, Madrid, Manchester, Marseille, Milan, Nantes, Naples, Nice, Palermo, Paris, Pau, Périgueux, Perpignan, Quimper, Rimini, Rome, St Étienne, Strasbourg, Toulouse, Vannes, Venice and Verona.

Fleet (28): 15 x ATR42-500, 7 x Canadair Regional Jet 100ER, 5 x Fokker 70, 1 x Fokker 100. *On order:* 7 x Canadair Regional Jet.

Colour scheme: Air Littoral introduced a new corporate identity during 1996, to underscore its desire to redefine itself and its image as a 'company of the South'. The white fuselage is adorned with colourful designs in blue, yellow and red, including a striking interpretation of migratory birds flying against the blue skies covering the nose of the aircraft. Sun, stars, flowers and leaves are interwoven into a novel tailfin design. Unusually bold 'AIR LITTORAL' titles are painted at the rear of the fuselage in blue.

Illustrated: Air Littoral has modernised its entire fleet, including a large number of the latest ATR42-500 twin-turboprop.

AIR MALTA (KM/AMC)

Founded/First Service: 30 March 1973/1 April 1974
Base: Malta International Airport, Gudja, Malta
Services: Scheduled passenger and cargo flights to Amsterdam, Athens, Bahrain, Barcelona, Berlin, Birmingham, Brussels, Budapest, Cairo, Casablanca, Catania, Damascus, Dubai, Dublin, Düsseldorf, Frankfurt, Geneva, Glasgow, Hamburg, Istanbul, Larnaca, Lisbon, London, Lyon, Madrid, Manchester, Marseille, Milan, Monastir, Munich, Oslo, Palermo, Paris Orly, Rome, Stockholm, Tel Aviv, Tunis, Vienna and Zürich. A dedicated freighter service with a leased Boeing 727-200 between Malta and Brussels. Scheduled helicopter service links Malta with the neighbouring island of Gozo.
Fleet (11): 2 x Airbus A320-200, 2 x Boeing 737-200A, 3 x Boeing 737-300, 4 x Avro RJ70.
Colour scheme: The Air Malta corporate symbol is the eight-pointed, four-armed Maltese Cross, representing the four Christian values of prudence, justice, fortitude and temperance. It is displayed in white on a red field, covering the upper two thirds of the tailfin and underscored by three solid blue stripes, also carried along a predominantly white fuselage, which allude to the islands of Malta, Gozo and Comino. The Maltese Cross is also repeated on the engines. The red Air Malta logotype is applied in a Roman typeface. This corporate identity was introduced in 1989.

Illustrated: Air Malta began Airbus A320 services to European cities in early September 1990. They are operated in a mixed Club and Economy configuration.

AIR MAURITIUS (MK/MAU)

Founded/First Service: 14 June 1967/August 1972
Base: Sir Seewoosagur Ramgoolam Airport, Plaine Magnien, Mauritius
Services: International and regional flights to Amsterdam (cargo only), Antananarivo, Bombay (joint service with Air India), Brussels, Durban, Frankfurt (with Lufthansa), Geneva, Harare, Hong Kong (with Cathay Pacific), Johannesburg, Kuala Lumpur, London, Melbourne, Moroni, Munich (with Lufthansa), Nairobi, Paris, Perth, Réunion, Rome, Singapore, Vienna and Zürich.
Fleet (10): 4 x Airbus A340-300, 2 x ATR42-300, 2 x Bell 206B JetRanger, 2 x Boeing 767-200ER.
On order: 2 x Airbus A340-300.
Colour scheme: A bright red windowline, trimmed below with a pinstripe in the same colour, runs the whole length of the aircraft, finished in white down to wing level. Upper case 'AIR MAURITIUS' titles are promoted alongside the national flag on the forward fuselage. The national flag, adopted on independence in 1968, features four colours: red for the martyrs of independence, blue for the sea, yellow for freedom and green for its fertile soil. The airline's red *paille en queue* (a tropical bird) symbol flies across a white band on a quartered, largely red tail.
Illustrated: Air Mauritius introduced the Airbus A340-300 in May 1994, serving its intercontinental routes. It features 301 seats in a spacious three-class accommodation.

AIR NAMIBIA (SW/NMB)

Founded/First Service: 1946 as South West Air Transport, present title adopted October 1991

Base: Eros and J. G. Strijdom Airports, Windhoek, Namibia

Services: Regional and domestic services, together with long-haul flights to Frankfurt and London from Windhoek. Local flights serve Livingstone and Lusaka, Zambia; Victoria Falls and Harare, Zimbabwe; Maun, Botswana; and Cape Town and Johannesburg, South Africa. Eleven domestic points are also on the schedule, serving among others the country's impressive tourist destinations.

Fleet (7): 1 x Boeing 737-200, 2 x 747SP, 3 x Beech 1900C, 1 x Cessna 414A Chancellor.

Colour scheme: A broad 'straight through' yellow windowline is flanked top and bottom by thinner dark blue cheatlines. The white tailfin is dominated by a large encircled yellow sun through which flies a flamingo. The national flag is displayed at the top of the fin and 'Air Namibia' titles in dark blue on the white fuselage ahead of the wing. The national flag was adopted following the country's independence in 1990.

Illustrated: Air Namibia uses two Boeing 747SPs, operated on lease from South African Airways. They fly the airline's long-haul services to Frankfurt and London.

AIR NEW ZEALAND (NZ/ANZ)

Founded/First Service: 1939 as TEAL/30 April 1940, present name adopted 1 April 1965

Base: Auckland International Airport, Auckland, New Zealand

Services: International flag services from Auckland, Wellington and Christchurch across the Tasman Sea to Adelaide, Brisbane, Cairns, Melbourne, Perth and Sydney, and to Apia, Bangkok, Denpasar, Frankfurt, Fukuoka, Hong Kong, Honolulu, London, Los Angeles, Nadi, Nagoya, Norfolk Island, Noumea, Osaka, Papeete, Rarotonga, Seoul, Taipei, Tokyo, Tonga, Toronto and Vancouver. Also serves main 24 domestic points, as well as subsidiary services, provided under the Air New Zealand Link title by Air Nelson and Eagle Airways.

Fleet (33): 12 x Boeing 737-200A, 5 x 747-200B, 5 x 747-400, 5 x 767-200ER, 6 x 767-300ER.

On order: 6 x Boeing 737-300, 1 x 747-400, 1 x 767-300ER.

Colour scheme: The introduction of a bold new livery in April 1996 reflects the airline's desire to position itself as a world leader in air travel to and within the South Pacific. One of the key elements is the 'Pacific wave' in blue and turquoise, running through deep blue 'AIR NEW ZEALAND' titling on a clean white fuselage, symbolising the meeting of sea and shore around the islands of the Pacific. The deep blue tailfin bears in white a redesigned koru, the strong, curved spiral that dominated the beautifully etched canoe prows and signifies new life and replenishment.

Illustrated: The first aircraft in Air New Zealand's new colours was the 747-400. It joined the fleet from December 1989 and operates all long-haul services.

AIR SEYCHELLES (HM/SEY)

Founded/First Service: 15 September 1977 as Seychelles Airlines, present title adopted March 1979

Base: Seychelles International Airport, Victoria, Mahé, Seychelles

Services: International passenger services from Mahé to Bombay, Dubai, Frankfurt, Johannesburg, London Gatwick, Madrid, Manchester, Nairobi, Paris, Rome, Singapore and Zürich. Also domestic inter-island flights between Mahé, Praslin, Frégate, Bird, Denis and Desroches. Main domestic shuttle provides more than 20 daily flights on the 15min Mahé-Praslin link.

Fleet (7): 1 x Boeing 767-200ER, 1 x 767-300ER, 4 x DHC-6 Twin Otter 300, 1 x Pilatus Britten-Norman BN-2A Islander.

Colour scheme: A pair of pure white fairy terns, flying in harmony against the background of the red and green colours of the Seychelles flag, is the airline's symbol applied to the tailfin of its aircraft. The lower green is preceded by three graduated diagonal stripes wrapped over the top of the all-white fuselage. The symbol is also applied to the engine cowlings. Blue 'Air Seychelles' titles are displayed on the upper fuselage together with the national flag, whose broad red band of revolution and progress, and lower green alluding to its people's reliance on agriculture, enclose a white wavy stripe which symbolises the resources of the Indian Ocean where the islands are located.

Illustrated: Air Seychelles' Boeing 767-200ER flies to destinations in Europe and Asia. It is configured in a two-class layout featuring 12 Pearl (Business) Class and 196 Economy Class seats.

AIRTOURS INTERNATIONAL (VZ/AIH)

Founded/First Service: 1990/11 March 1991
Base: Manchester International Airport, Manchester, Lancashire, United Kingdom
Services: Inclusive tour services to Europe and all the Mediterranean holiday resorts, as well as further afield to the Caribbean, the United States, The Gambia and Australia, serving Orlando, Las Vegas, Barbados, Grand Cayman, Varadero (Cuba), Montego Bay (Jamaica), Antigua and Banjul. UK departure points are London Gatwick, Belfast, Birmingham, Bristol, Cardiff, East Midlands, Glasgow, Humberside, Leeds/Bradford, Manchester and Newcastle.
Fleet (18): 10 x Airbus A320-200, 6 x Boeing 757-200, 2 x 767-300E.
On order: 1 x Boeing 757-200, 1 x 767-300ER.
Colour scheme: Airtours' present identity was introduced in 1995. Its aircraft feature a royal blue belly and tail over a white fuselage, distinguished by a jade fuselage stripe and horizontal and vertical tail flashes in jade, orange and yellow, representing the group colours. The airline name appears in italicised lettering on the forward fuselage.
Illustrated: Airtours International utilises the extended-range Boeing 767-300ER on its high-density long-haul flights, fitted out for 326 passengers in an all-Economy layout.

AIR TRANSAT (TS/TSC)

Founded/First Service: December 1986
Base: Montreal International Airport, Mirabel, Québec, Canada
Services: Regular and ad hoc charter services from Montreal, Toronto and Québec City to Mexico, the Caribbean, United States, Central and South America, and across the North Atlantic to Europe. Main European countries served are France and the United Kingdom, including Glasgow, Leeds/Bradford, London, Lyon, Manchester, Marseille, Newcastle, Nice, Paris and Toulouse. Amsterdam, Athens, Frankfurt, Madrid and Rome also frequently served.
Fleet (11): 4 x Boeing 757-200, 7 x Lockheed L1011 TriStar 1.
Colour scheme: A broad royal blue windowline is underscored by a similarly coloured thinner line which separates the upper white fuselage from the partially metal/grey underbelly. The blue windowline broadens at the rear and sweeps up to cover most of the tailfin, which also features a wide red band starting at the tailplane. White, lower case 'at' initials are set into the blue on the upper part of the fin, and repeated on the engine cowlings. 'air transat' titles in royal blue — with the exception of the last letter 'a' which is in red — are displayed on the forward upper fuselage.
Illustrated: Air Transat's Lockheed TriStars operate on the airline's long-haul routes across the North Atlantic to Europe. They are configured in an all-Tourist layout for 340 passengers. *Alan J. Wright*

AIR UK (UK/UKA)

Founded/First Service: 16 January 1980 through merger of Air Anglia, British Island Airways, Air West and Air Wales

Base: London Stansted Airport, Stansted, Essex, United Kingdom

Services: Scheduled passenger services within the UK, and to Europe serving Amsterdam, Bergen, Brussels, Copenhagen, Düsseldorf, Florence, Frankfurt, Hamburg, Maastricht/Aachen, Madrid, Milan, Munich, Paris, Prague, Stavanger and Zürich. Air UK operates from all three London airports of Heathrow, Gatwick and Stansted.

Fleet (37): 1 x British Aerospace 146-100, 10 x 146-300, 9 x Fokker 50, 11 x Fokker 100, 1 x Fokker F27-200, 5 x F27-500.

Colour scheme: The colour scheme was modified with the delivery of the Fokker 100s in July 1992. It now comprises more elegant triple cheatlines in two shades of blue, a light blue line being sandwiched between two varying thickness bands of deep blue. Starting just under the cockpit, they sweep up at the rear to form a deep blue fin, while the light blue forms the 'hoist' on which flutters half a Union Flag. 'Air UK' titles appear behind the forward passenger door in deep blue.

Illustrated: The four-engined British Aerospace 146-300 forms the mainline fleet of expanding Air UK.

AIR ZIMBABWE (UM/AZW)

Founded/First Service: 1 September 1967 as Air Rhodesia, present title adopted in April 1980.

Base: Harare Airport, Harare, Zimbabwe

Services: Long-haul services to Sydney via Perth in conjunction with Qantas, and to European destinations including London Gatwick and Frankfurt via Larnaca. Also flies regional routes in Southern and East Africa, serving Durban, Johannesburg, Gaborone, Manzini, Maputo, Lusaka, Nairobi, Lilongwe, Dar es Salaam, Mauritius and Windhoek, together with an eight-point domestic network, principally to the country's tourist resorts.

Fleet (10): 2 x Boeing 707-320B, 3 x 737-200A, 2 x 767-200ER, 1 x British Aerospace 146-200, 2 x Fokker 50.

Colour scheme: A quadruple cheatline of the national colours of green, yellow, red and black on a white upper fuselage, produces an exciting colour scheme. Commencing at the nose, the stripes step up in broader diagonal bands to the windowline, ultimately embracing most of the tailfin. Near the top of the fin appears the Zimbabwe bird, a soapstone carving of an ancient African culture, fronting the red star of socialism and national aspiration. 'air zimbabwe' titles are displayed alongside a fluttering portrayal of the national flag.

Illustrated: Air Zimbabwe has been operating the twin-engined extended-range Boeing 767-200 on its European routes since November 1989.

Chris Doggett/F. Stop International

ALITALIA (AZ/AZA)

Founded/First Service: 16 September 1946/May 1947
Base: Leonardo da Vinci Airport (Fiumicino), Rome, Italy
Services: International flights to 109 cities on all continents, with a strong emphasis on Europe, where it serves most major cities, and the Americas, linking Rome with Boston, Bogotá, Buenos Aires, Caracas, Chicago, Lima, Los Angeles, Mexico City, Miami, Montreal, New York, Rio de Janeiro, Santiago, Santo Domingo, São Paulo and Toronto. Also domestic network flown in its own colours and those of subsidiary Avianova.
Fleet (152): 14 x Airbus A300B4-100/200, 13 x A321-100,
11 x Boeing 747-200B/(SCD), 5 x 767-300(ER), 11 x McDonnell Douglas DC-9-32,
90 x MD-82, 3 x MD-11, 5 x MD-11CF.
Avianova: 9 x ATR42-300, 4 x ATR72-200, 5 x Fokker 70.
On order: 27 x Airbus A321-100.
Colour scheme: Alitalia's striking corporate image in the national colours was designed by Walter Landor Associates and adopted fleetwide in January 1971. It focuses on a bold stylised 'A' in green with a red centre, which fills the tailfin as a continuation of a green windowline, fading to a point towards the nose. The 'A' is repeated as the first letter in the black italic logotype on the all-white fuselage.
The European Union flag precedes the name and is repeated behind the aircraft registration. The Avianova livery is closely based on Alitalia's, using the same colours, but with slight differences in the letter 'A' in the title.
Illustrated: The most recent arrival is the extended-range Boeing 767-300 being leased from Ansett. It is used on long-haul services in a two-class layout for 241 passengers.

ALL NIPPON AIRWAYS — ANA (NH/ANH)

Founded/First Service: December 1957 through merger of JHAT and Far East Airlines
Base: Narita Airport, Tokyo, Japan
Services: Comprehensive domestic network linking more than 30 cities on all Japanese islands with high-frequency services. Since 1986 also international routes now serving Bangkok, Beijing, Brisbane, Dalian, Guam, Hong Kong, Kuala Lumpur, Los Angeles, New York, Qingdao, Seoul, Shanghai, Singapore, Sydney and Washington, as well as Frankfurt, London, Moscow, Paris, Rome and Vienna in Europe.
Fleet (132): 23 x Airbus A320-200, 6 x 747-200B, 14 x 747SR-100, 19 x 747-400, 25 x 767-200, 38 x 767-300, 7 x 777-200.
On order: 10 x Airbus A321-100, 5 x A340-300, 2 x Boeing 747-400, 4 x 767-300, 11 x 777-200, 10 x 777-300.
Colour scheme: An angular cheatline in two shades of blue broadens along the white upper fuselage until it takes over the whole of the tail, incorporating the 'ANA' logo in white. The logo also appears in Japanese on both sides of the fuselage near the front passenger door and is preceded by the *hi-no-maru*, or sun disk of the national flag. The livery was introduced in 1983 with the delivery of the Boeing 767s.
Illustrated: ANA's Boeing-dominated fleet includes the Boeing 747-400, some of which are operated on the busiest domestic routes in a high-density configuration for 569 passengers.

AMERICAN AIRLINES (AA/AAL)

Founded/First Service: 13 May 1934, predecessor companies go back to 15 April 1926
Base: Dallas/Fort Worth Airport, Texas, USA
Services: Extensive US domestic network with hubs at Dallas/Fort Worth, Chicago, Miami and San Juan, connecting also with feeder services operated by American Eagle, American's regional airline affiliate. International schedules to Canada, Mexico, the Caribbean, Japan, and to Europe, now serving Birmingham, Brussels, Frankfurt, Glasgow, London Heathrow and Gatwick, Madrid, Manchester, Milan Malpensa, Paris Orly, Stockholm and Zürich.
Fleet (649): 35 x Airbus A300-600R, 81 x 727-200A, 90 x 757-200, 8 x 767-200, 22 x 767-200ER, 41 x 767-300ER, 75 x Fokker 100,
16 x McDonnell Douglas DC-10-10ER, 4 x DC-10-30, 17 x MD-11, 250 x MD-82, 10 x MD-83.
On order: 75 x 737-600/700/800, 12 x 757-200, 4 x 767-300ER, 12 x 777.
Colour scheme: Highly-polished natural metal fuselage and tail finish provides the backdrop for a 'straight-through' patriotic triple cheatline in red, white and blue. The long-established motif of a blue eagle swoops down between the twin peaks of the double red and blue 'A' initials, outlined in white. 'AMERICAN' lettering in red, again with a white outline, is displayed on the cabin roof. The livery was adopted in 1969.
Illustrated: The three-engined McDonnell Douglas MD-11, together with the Boeing 767, serve American's trans-Atlantic network.

AMERICAN TRANS AIR (TZ/AMT)

Founded/First Service: March 1981
Base: Indiana International Airport, Indianapolis, Indiana, USA
Services: Scheduled and charter service for leisure travellers from Boston, Chicago, Milwaukee, Indianapolis and Philadelphia to several Florida destinations including Fort Lauderdale, Fort Myers, Orlando, St Petersburg and Sarasota/Bradenton, and to Las Vegas and Phoenix. Additionally, strong charter-only business within the United States, to the Caribbean and across the North Atlantic to Europe.
Fleet (51): 20 x Boeing 727-200A, 14 x 757-200,
6 x Lockheed L1011 TriStar 1, 11 x L1011 TriStar 50.
On order: 2 x Boeing 757-200.
Colour scheme: American Trans Air adopted a new colour scheme in early 1996, to identify itself more closely with its leisure business. Its largely white aircraft are now dominated by a painting style tailfin, featuring a palm tree, bright sun, magenta waves and the airline initials on a midnight blue background. The underbelly is painted in the same deep blue, as are the engine cowlings, both decorated with similar motifs. Huge blue and gold 'ATA' initials cover the forward fuselage.
Illustrated: Lockheed L1011 from the American Trans Air fleet.

AUSTRIAN AIRLINES (OS/AUA)

Founded/First Service: 30 September 1957/31 March 1958
Base: Vienna International Airport, Schwechat, Austria
Services: Scheduled passenger and cargo services to 80 cities in 45 countries throughout Europe and to the Middle and Far East, North America and South Africa. Long-haul destinations are Almaty, Amman, Beijing, Damascus, Dhahran, Johannesburg, New York, Osaka, Riyadh, Tehran, Tokyo and Washington DC. Particularly strong coverage of Central and Eastern Europe. Charter flights by subsidiary, Austrian Air Transport.
Fleet (34): 2 x A340-200, 4 x Airbus A310-300, 4 x A321-100, 4 x Fokker 70, 7 x McDonnell Douglas MD-81, 6 x MD-82, 2 x MD-83, 2 x MD-87ER, 3 x MD-87SR.
On order: 7 x Airbus A320-200, 2 x A321-100.
Colour scheme: After only minimal changes in the first 20 years, the airline launched a major redesign on 4 October 1995. Designed by GGK Vienna and UK consultants Davies and Barron, the new colour scheme connects the national colours of red, white and red on the tailfin with the colours of Austria's landscape, the green of woods and meadows and the blue of rivers and lakes, achieved by a blue/green colour line under the windows. The famous red arrow symbol has been retained as an element of continuity, and is set into the centre of the tail and ahead of the anthracite grey 'AUSTRIAN AIRLINES' titles, which provides a contrast to the Alpine white fuselage, representing the country's mountains, glaciers and snow.

Illustrated: Austrian Airlines took delivery of its first Airbus A321-100 in January 1996.

AVIANCA COLOMBIA (AV/AVA)

Founded/First Service: 5 December 1919 as SCADTA/12 September 1920. Present name adopted 14 June 1940

Base: Eldorado International Airport, Bogota, Colombia

Services: Extensive domestic network and scheduled flights throughout Latin America, Caribbean, the United States and Europe. Destinations include Aruba, Buenos Aires, Cancun, Caracas, Curaçao, Frankfurt, Guatemala City, Lima, Los Angeles, Madrid, Manaus, Mexico City, Miami, Montevideo, New York, Panama City, Paris, Port au Prince, Quito, Rio de Janeiro, San José, Santiago de Chile and Santo Domingo.

Fleet (29): 2 x Boeing 727-200A, 3 x 757-200, 2 x 767-200ER, 1 x 767-300ER, 10 x Fokker 50, 11 x McDonnell Douglas MD-83.

Colour scheme: The upper half of the fuselage is painted in a warm red, falling away from a complete coverage at the nose to above the windowline at the rear and continuing up the back of the tail. 'Avianca Colombia' titles are set into the red field in white and black respectively. Red 'Avianca' lettering colours the white section of the fin.

Illustrated: In December 1980, Avianca became the first South American airline to order the Boeing 767 twinjet. Two 767-200 Extended Range (ER) models entered service during 1990 and are used principally on routes to North America.

BALKAN BULGARIAN AIRLINES (LZ/LAZ)

Founded/First Service: 29 June 1947/12 September 1947 as TABSO, present title adopted in 1968
Base: Sofia International Airport, Sofia, Bulgaria
Services: Domestic and international passenger and cargo services to points in Europe, the United States, Africa and the Middle and Far East. Destinations include Amsterdam, Bahrain, Bangkok, Beirut, Cairo, Casablanca, Frankfurt, Harare, Johannesburg, Kuwait, Lagos, Malta, New York, Paris, Rome, Tel Aviv, Tunis, Vienna and Zürich.
Fleet (58): 3 x Airbus A320-200, 3 x Antonov An-12F, 14 x An-24V,
3 x Boeing 737-500, 2 x 767-200ER, 2 x Ilyushin IL-18D, 4 x IL-18V,
5 x Tupolev Tu-134A-3, 15 x Tu-154B-2, 7 x Tu-154M.
Colour scheme: Narrow twin cheatlines in the national colours of red and mid-green flow along the pure white fuselage, wrapping around the belly of the aircraft behind the wing. Red and green brush strokes on the white tail add a fresh, modern look. Bold red 'Balkan' titles are applied in English on the starboard side and in Bulgarian on port, midway on the cabin roof behind the 'shooting star' emblem. These are followed by smaller 'Bulgarian Airlines' subtitles in green. The present scheme was adopted in late 1985.
Illustrated: Although Balkan's mainline fleet now comprises Boeing aircraft, it still retains a large number of ex-Soviet aircraft, including this Ilyushin IL-18V.

BIMAN BANGLADESH AIRLINES (BG/BBC)

Founded/First Service: 4 January 1972/February 1972

Base: Zia International Airport, Dhaka, Bangladesh

Services: Scheduled services from the capital Dhaka to 27 international destinations in 21 countries, including Abu Dhabi, Bahrain, Bangkok, Bombay (Mumbai), Brussels, Calcutta, Delhi, Dhahran, Dubai, Doha, Frankfurt, Hong Kong, Jeddah, Karachi, Kathmandu, Kuala Lumpur, Kuwait, London, Muscat, New York, Paris, Rome, Riyadh, Singapore, Sharjah, Tokyo and Yangon. Also domestic flights to seven major cities.

Fleet (11): 2 x Airbus A310-300, 2 x BAe ATP, 2 x Fokker F28-4000 Fellowship, 5 x McDonnell Douglas DC-10-30.

Colour scheme: The national colours of red and dark green are used in the form of a cheatline running at window level the whole length of the all-white fuselage, cut to a fine point at the front. Dark green 'BANGLADESH AIRLINES' titles are carried in English and Bengali on the port and starboard side respectively, preceded by the national flag. A white stork, flying across a rising sun represented by a crimson disk, is positioned centrally between horizontal fin bands in red and green and on the engine cowlings. The livery was introduced in 1983 with the delivery of the DC-10s.

Illustrated: The Airbus A310-300 is the latest addition to the fleet, the two aircraft being delivered in June and August 1996, taking over from the McDonnell Douglas DC-10-30 on regional flights to the Middle East and South East Asia.

BRAATHENS SAFE (BU/BRA)

Founded/First Service: 26 March 1946/December 1946
Base: Oslo Fornebu Airport, Oslo, Norway
Services: Biggest domestic operator in Norway, serving 15 major cities, including Alesund, Bergen, Bodo, Harstad/Narvik, Haugesund, Kristiansand, Kristiansund, Molde, Oslo, Roros, Sandjeford, Stavanger, Svalbard (Spitzbergen), Tromso and Trondheim, with operations centred on Oslo, Bergen and Trondheim. International scheduled flights to Alicante, Billund, Jersey, London Gatwick, Malaga, Newcastle, Rome and Stockholm. Murmansk served in association with Aeroflot. Also European charter flights.
Fleet (29): 6 x Boeing 737-400, 23 x 737-500.
On order: 6 x Boeing 737-700.
Colour scheme: Braathens' aircraft are painted in Arctic white, with the only other colours being the red and blue of the national flag, which is painted on the tailfin. The flag is indicative of Norway's long subjugation to Denmark, with the red and white *Dannebrog* used as a base, but overlaid with a blue cross. A thin blue cheatline topped by a broad red band extends throughout the length of the fuselage. The airline title is applied forward in capital letters and in a matching blue. All aircraft are named after Norse heroes, who are depicted in a wooden frieze on the forward bulkhead inside the cabin.
Illustrated: Braathens SAFE operates an all Boeing 737 twinjet fleet, dominated by the smallest version, the 737-500, typically fitted out for 119 passengers.

BRIT AIR (DB/BZH)

Founded/First Service: 1973
Base: Aérodrome de Ploujean, Morlaix, Brittany, France
Services: Scheduled domestic services within metropolitan France, linking Brest, Caen, Le Havre, Limoges and Rennes to Lyon; Paris Charles de Gaulle and Orly, Nice and Toulouse to Rennes; and seasonally between Deauville and Nice. Cross-border European services from Brest, Nantes, Rennes, Le Havre, Caen and Rouen, plus Quimper in summer to London Gatwick; and Toulouse to Southampton and Brussels. Also flights on behalf of the Air France Group.
Fleet (21): 2 x ATR72-100, 10 x ATR42-300, 9 x Canadair Regional Jet 100ER.
Colour scheme: The new corporate identity provides a clean modern look, highlighted by an overall white fuselage, 'BRIT AIR' titles near the front and on the engine cowlings, and the company symbol applied on the vertical tailfin and, on a smaller scale, below the rear cockpit window. This comprises two elements: Triskele, a Celtic symbol representing the three elements of earth, fire and water,

BRITANNIA AIRWAYS (BY/BAL)

Founded/First Service: 1 December 1961/5 May 1962 as Euravia (London), present title adopted 16 August 1964
Base: London Luton Airport, Luton, Bedfordshire, United Kingdom
Services: Inclusive-tour charter flights from Luton, London Gatwick, Manchester, Birmingham and some 14 other provincial UK airports to more than 100 regular destinations throughout Europe and the Mediterranean countries, taking in all the main holiday resort areas of Portugal, Spain, Italy, Greece, Turkey, Tunisia, Malta and the Canary Islands. Also long-haul routes to the Maldives, India, South Africa, Australia, New Zealand, Canada, United States, Mexico and the Caribbean.
Fleet (28): 5 x Boeing 757-200ER, 14 x 757-200, 6 x 767-200ER, 3 x 767-300ER.
On order: 5 x 767-300ER.
Colour scheme: A patriotic livery with deep-blue full-length stripes beginning at the belly of the aircraft and graduating to a pinstripe as they approach the windowline. The blue is trimmed with narrow red and gold bands. The white upper fuselage displays strong 'Britannia' lettering and Queen Boadicea's

BRITISH MIDLAND AIRWAYS (BD/BMA)

Founded/First Service: 1938 as Air Schools, present title adopted 1964
Base: East Midlands Airport, Castle Donington, Derbyshire, United Kingdom
Services: Scheduled passenger flights serving Aberdeen, Amsterdam, Belfast, Bergen, Birmingham, Brussels, Copenhagen, Dublin, East Midlands, Edinburgh, Frankfurt, Glasgow, Leeds Bradford, Malaga, Nice, Palma, Paris, Prague, Teesside and Zürich. Many destinations served from London Heathrow where the airline is the second largest carrier after British Airways. Connections to Jersey in the Channel Islands scheduled from most major UK airports.
Fleet (36): 5 x Boeing 737-300, 6 x 737-400, 14 x 737-500, 2 x BAe ATP, 1 x BAe Jetstream 41, 4 x Fokker 70, 4 x Fokker 100.
Colour scheme: British Midland unveiled an update of its products and aircraft livery on 30 September 1996. Midnight blue and red cheatlines now separate the pale grey underside of the aircraft from the deep blue cabin roof. New 'British Midland' titles in white upper and lower case lettering are applied alongside the red 'BM' motif which is partially striated to give the appearance of speed. The 'M' is crowned

and Ermine, the emblem of Britanny. Colours were selected from the region's natural environment, including the yellow of broom for Triskele, the white of the Breton flag as the main colour of the aircraft, and European blue for Ermine and airline titles, replacing the black to provide a brighter effect.

Illustrated: The 50-seat Canadair Regional Jet now flies main domestic and European services.

helmeted head in blue outlined in red. The warrior queen, carrying a trident and holding the Union Flag shield, sits on the blue tail above reversed pinstripes. The livery was created by London design house Peter Eaton and Partners and implemented in 1983.

Illustrated: Flagships of the fleet are three brand-new Boeing 767-300ERs, delivered to the airline in May 1996.

with a white diamond, alluding to the airline's inflight Diamond Service. The words 'The Airline of Europe' have also been added. The 'BM' motif dominates the tailfin as before.

Illustrated: Following the withdrawal of the last DC-9, the mainline fleet now comprises three models of the Boeing 737, including the smallest 737-500.

BRITISH AIRWAYS (BA/BAW)

Founded/First Service: 31 March 1924 as Imperial Airways, present title adopted 1 April 1972

Bases: London Heathrow and Gatwick Airports, United Kingdom

Services: Largest global network of any airline, with scheduled passenger and cargo services linking the UK with 170 cities in 80 countries on all continents. Also comprehensive domestic network serving 15 destinations, including the main 'Super Shuttle' services from London to Manchester, Glasgow, Edinburgh, Belfast and Newcastle, the Scottish Highlands and Islands routes and regional flights. Regional operations by subsidiaries Brymon Airways, Deutsche BA and TAT European Airlines, and franchisees CityFlyer Express, Loganair, British Regional Airlines, GB Airways, Maersk Air UK, Sun-Air of Scandinavia and Comair (South Africa).

Fleet (252): 6 x Aerospatiale/BAC Concorde, 5 x Airbus A320-100, 5 x A320-200, 35 x Boeing 737-200, 37 x 737-400, 15 x 747-100, 16 x 747-200B(SCD), 34 x 747-400, 43 x 757-200, 24 x 767-300ER, 10 x 777-200, 14 x BAe ATP, 8 x McDonnell Douglas DC-10-30.

On order: 16 x Boeing 747-400, 5 x 777-200.

Colour scheme: The British Airways corporate identity was designed by Landor Associates and unveiled in December 1984. It has been designed around three colours: pearl grey, rich midnight blue and Speedwing red. The Speedbird, in use since the days of Imperial Airways, was the inspiration behind the dramatic red Speedwing, which provides an essential

link between the nose and the fin of the aircraft and forms a close relationship with the stylised Union Jack. The tailfin is divided into two halves, with the upper in midnight blue promoting the coat of arms in grey above a quartered Union Jack, set into the lower pearl grey. The 'BRITISH AIRWAYS' titles, in a bold Optima typeface, are traditionally placed and aligned with the red Speedwing, which runs almost the full length of the fuselage, providing a bold separation between the pearl grey top and midnight blue lower fuselage and engine nacelles. Slight variations exist within the Concorde fleet. Concorde has an equally distinctive all-white fuselage in order to reflect the heat and keep to a minimum the extremely high surface temperatures generated in supersonic flight. The coat of arms was granted to British Airways in January 1975, in recognition of its service to the nation. Prepared by York Herald of Arms, Dr Conrad Swan, it was inspired in part by the Union Jack which is recognised all over the world as representative of Great Britain. The shield is supported by Pegasus, the winged horse, and a lion guardant winged at the shoulders. Above the shield is the helm and crest, consisting of a sunburst symbolic of energy, strength and vitality, rising from an astral crown. The motto is 'To Fly to Serve'. British Airways colours are also carried by aircraft operated by its subsidiaries and franchisees. British Airways is currently updating its corporate identity and a final version is expected sometime during 1997.

Illustrated: A British Airways Boeing 747-400 an interim livery (above). More and more small regional aircraft are appearing in the British Airways livery, including this DHC-8-300 operated by Brymon Airways (opposite top). *SPA Photography*

BWIA INTERNATIONAL (BW/BWA)

Founded/First Service: 27 November 1939

Base: Piarco Airport, Port of Spain, Trinidad and Tobago

Services: Passenger and cargo flights throughout the Caribbean islands and to Caracas, Miami, New York and Toronto. Trans-Atlantic services link Frankfurt, London and Zürich with direct flights to Antigua and Barbados, with onward connections to Port of Spain. London and Frankfurt also have direct connections to St Lucia.

Fleet (13): 2 x Airbus A321-100, 4 x Lockheed L1011 TriStar 500, 7 x McDonnell Douglas MD-83.

Colour scheme: BWIA modernised its corporate identity with the delivery of its first Airbus A321. Its golden 'sand' cheatline above a Caribbean blue sky pinstripe has been replaced with broad golden yellow and turquoise bands which separate the upper white fuselage from the lower grey. Both widen at the rear, with the turquoise band wrapped around the underside of the rear fuselage, while the yellow fills most of the tailfin and is interrupted only by the company's sun symbol in turquoise and gold, broken by magenta 'BWIA' initials. The turquoise line broadens out at the rear and wraps under the fuselage.

'BWIA International' titles cover the forward fuselage, ahead of the national flag and the words 'We are the Caribbean'. The lettering is in black with the exception of the 'BWIA' initials which are again in magenta.

Illustrated: BWIA's first A321-100 entered service on the route from Port of Spain to New York, via Antigua, on 13 July 1996.

CALEDONIAN AIRWAYS (KT/BKT)

Founded/First Service: 10 December 1987
Base: London Gatwick Airport, Crawley, West Sussex, United Kingdom
Services: Holiday charters to the traditional Mediterranean market, plus long-haul flying to destinations as far afield as Barbados, Jamaica, the Dominican Republic, the United States, Kenya, Goa and the Maldives. All the most popular destinations in Spain, Greece, Portugal, Morocco, Tunisia, Italy, Turkey and the Canary Islands are in the summer programme.
Fleet (10): 3 x Airbus A320-200, 5 x Lockheed L1011-100 TriStar,
2 x McDonnell Douglas DC-10-30.
Colour scheme: The Caledonian Airways fleet combines the best of both British Airways and the former British Caledonian Airways, although the airline is now owned by Inspirations. The fuselage features the pearl grey upper and midnight blue under side of the former with the red speedwing replaced by a narrow gold cheatline. The tailfin displays the familiar lion rampant of BCal in the standard blue and gold arrangement. The word 'CALEDONIAN' is reproduced on the cabin roof in the same Optima typeface as British Airways.
Illustrated: Caledonian's long-haul flights are now shared between the Lockheed TriStar and the McDonnell Douglas DC-10-30 pictured.

CANADIAN AIRLINES INTERNATIONAL (CP/CDN)

Founded/First Service: January 1987 through merger of CP Air, Pacific Western Airlines, Nordair and Eastern Provincial Airways. Wardair acquired in 1990.

Bases: Calgary, Toronto and Vancouver International Airports, Canada

Services: Canada's largest domestic network, together with long-haul services to Bangkok, Beijing, Hong Kong, Honolulu, London, Los Angeles, Manila, Mexico City, Monterey, Nagoya, Rome, San Francisco, São Paulo, Taipei and Tokyo. Global code-share alliances with American Airlines, British Airways, Qantas, Air New Zealand, Alitalia, Mandarin Airlines, Philippine Airlines and Varig. An extensive local commuter network, operated by Canadian Regional Airlines right across Canada and to the USA.

Fleet (92): 12 x Airbus A320-200, 46 x Boeing 737-200 Advanced, 9 x 737-200 Combi, 4 x Boeing 747-400, 11 x 767-300ER, 10 x McDonnell Douglas DC-10-30ER.

Colour scheme: The Pacific blue belly of the aircraft is separated from the white cabin roof by straight-through pinstripe red and pewter cheatlines. The latter matches the expanded tail bars, which represent the five continents served and form the backdrop to the red wing symbol, formerly of Pacific Western. The cabin roof displays 'Canadian' titles in blue, with the penultimate character replaced by the company insignia, so that it can be read as either 'Canadian' or the French 'Canadien', without having to apply dual titling.

Illustrated: Canadian Airlines uses its twin-engined, General Electric CF6-80C2-powered Boeing 767-300ERs on ETOPS (Extended Range Twin Operations) on services across the North Atlantic to Europe, and to China, Mexico and Brazil.

CARGOLUX AIRLINES INTERNATIONAL (CV/CLX)

Founded/First Service: 4 March 1970
Base: Luxembourg (Findel) Airport, Grand Duchy of Luxembourg
Services: Regular all-cargo services between Europe, the Americas, Near and Middle East, Africa and Asia/Pacific, together with worldwide charter flights. Among regular destinations are Abu Dhabi, Athens, Bangkok, Beirut, Colombo, Damascus, Detroit, Dubai, Harare, Hong Kong, Houston, Istanbul, Johannesburg, Keflavik, Komatsu, Kuala Lumpur, Kuwait, Los Angeles, Madras, Mexico City, Miami, New York, San Francisco, Santiago de Chile, São Paulo, Seattle, Singapore, Skavsta and Taipei. Also offers maintenance and sub-leasing services, as well as CHAMP (Cargo Handling and Management Planning), the only fully-integrated cargo system in the world.
Fleet (7): 4 x Boeing 747-200F, 3 x 747-400F. *On order:* 2 x Boeing 747-400F.
Colour scheme: The light grey painted overall fuselage is highlighted by simple straight cheatlines using the blue, white and red tricolour of Luxembourg, broken on the forward fuselage by bold black 'cargolux' titling in lower case lettering. The airline's distinctive three-dimensional 'triple box' motif in red outlined in white, dominates the aircraft's massive tailfins.
Illustrated: Cargolux's all-Boeing fleet of freighters is headed by the latest 747-400F which can carry up to 129 tonnes of cargo.

CATHAY PACIFIC AIRWAYS (CX/CPA)

Founded/First Service: 24 September 1946

Base: Kai Tak International Airport, Hong Kong

Services: Scheduled passenger and cargo services to 44 destinations in 27 countries in the Far East Australasia, Europe, Africa and North America, plus another 11 in mainland China through associate Dragonair. Long-haul destinations are Adelaide, Amsterdam, Bahrain, Brisbane, Dubai, Frankfurt, Johannesburg, London, Los Angeles, Manchester, Melbourne, Paris, Perth, Rome, Sydney, Vancouver and Zürich.

Fleet (58): 10 x Airbus A330-300, 6 x A340-300, 7 x Boeing 747-200B, 4 x 747-200F, 6 x 747-300, 19 x 747-400, 2 x 747-400F, 4 x 777-200.

On order: 7 x Boeing 777-300.

Colour scheme: Centrepiece of the Landor Associates-designed identity is the 'brushwing' — a calligraphy stroke suggesting the wing of a bird — against a green background taking up most of the tailfin, and appearing in a similar arrangement under the cockpit. A red 'speed bar' encloses the bottom of the logo. The brushwing has been chosen to symbolise modern energy and confident elegance, representing the airline's well-won reputation for technical excellence and exacting standards of service. Together with the green 'CATHAY PACIFIC' titling in a unique typeface based on the arrow style on the shoulder of the aircraft, the image is said to have an oriental feel, while appealing to both its Asian and Western customers. The fuselage is largely grey, with a white roof from the windowline.

Illustrated: Cathay's Rolls-Royce Trent-powered Boeing 777 entered service on regional and Middle Eastern routes in May 1996.

CHINA AIRLINES (CI/CAL)

Founded/First Service: 16 December 1959
Base: Chiang Kai-Shek International Airport, Taipei, Taiwan
Services: International services to 29 cities, including Abu Dhabi, Amsterdam, Bangkok, Anchorage, Denpasar, Frankfurt, Fukuoka, Hanoi, Ho Chi Minh City, Hong Kong, Honolulu, Jakarta, Kuala Lumpur, Los Angeles, Manila, Nagoya, New York, Okinawa, Phuket, Rome, San Francisco, Singapore, Tokyo, Sydney, Vancouver and Zürich. Domestic services from Taipei to Kaohsiung. Also all-cargo flights to 17 destinations.
Fleet (40): 6 x Airbus A300-600R, 6 x A300B4-200, 3 x Boeing 737-200 Advanced, 2 x 737-400, 3 x 747-200B(SCD), 6 x 747-200F, 6 x 747-400, 4 x 747SP, 4 x McDonnell Douglas MD-11. Total of 47 new aircraft to be delivered by 2003.
Colour scheme: The new corporate identity, introduced on 7 October 1995, was developed by Singaporean consultancy Addison Design to illustrate the airline's commitments to sincerity, caring, innovation, sense of responsibility and the pursuit of excellence. The essence of the scheme is the pink plum blossom, the national flower of Taiwan, which adorns the tail of the aircraft, floating on a purple haze. The otherwise all-white aircraft features a two-tone blue chinstrap, with the upper lighter shade extending to the rear on the underside of the fuselage. Blue 'CHINA AIRLINES' titles are applied forward (on the Boeing 747 between the upper and main decks), with an abbreviated form in Chinese characters.
Illustrated: China Airlines' 411-seat Boeing 747-400 is scheduled on routes from Taipei to Hong Kong, Tokyo, Anchorage, Los Angeles and New York.

CHINA EASTERN AIRLINES (MU/CES)

Founded/First Service: 25 June 1988
Base: Hongqiao International Airport, Shanghai, People's Republic of China
Services: Trunk services to 43 cities in China from Shanghai, Nanjing, Hefei City, Nanchang and Qingdao, together with fast-expanding regional and long-haul network to Europe and the United States. International destinations are Bangkok, Brussels, Chicago, Fukuoka, Hong Kong, Los Angeles, Madrid, Nagasaki, Nagoya, Osaka, Seattle, Seoul, Singapore and Tokyo.
Fleet (76): 10 x Airbus A300-600R, 4 x A340-300, 3 x Antonov An-24V,
10 x Fokker 100, 5 x McDonnell Douglas MD-11, 1 x MD-11F, 13 x MD-82,
20 x Shijazhuang Y5, 10 x Xian Y7.
On order: 9 x McDonnell Douglas MD-90-30.
Colour scheme: China Eastern's aircraft are painted in white and grey, separated

CONDOR FLUGDIENST (DE/CFG)

Founded/First Service: 21 December 1955 as Deutsche Flugdienst/28 March 1956. Present name adopted 25 October 1961
Base: Frankfurt Rhein/Main Airport, Frankfurt, Germany
Services: Inclusive tour operations to more than 50 destinations in 34 countries. In addition to short-haul flights to the Mediterranean Basin, undertakes growing number of long-haul services from Frankfurt, Cologne/Bonn, Hannover and Munich to holiday resort areas in the Caribbean and Central America, East Africa and the Far East.
Fleet (37): 4 x Boeing 737-300, 1 x 747-430 (SCD), 18 x 757-200, 9 x 767-300ER,
5 x McDonnell Douglas DC-10-30.
On order: 6 x Airbus A320-200, 12 x Boeing 757-300.
Colour scheme: As a daughter company of German flag carrier Deutsche Lufthansa, Condor also uses the corporate blue and yellow colours, but in reverse. Its aircraft sport

CONTINENTAL AIRLINES (CO/COA)

Founded/First Service: 15 July 1934 as Varney Speed Lines, present title adopted 1 July 1937
Base: Houston Intercontinental Airport, Houston, Texas, USA
Services: Extensive network of scheduled passenger services to over 150 destinations within the United States, Central and South America, Mexico, the Caribbean, Far East, and London, Frankfurt, Madrid, Manchester and Paris in Europe. Three major traffic hubs are operated at Houston, Newark and Cleveland. Domestic feeder services are provided by wholly-owned subsidiary Continental Express, while affiliate Continental Micronesia, based in Guam, serves the Western Pacific islands.
Fleet (309): 31 x Boeing 727-200A, 12 x 737-100, 18 x 737-200, 65 x 737-300LR,
37 x 737-500, 2 x 747-200B, 24 x 757-200, 30 x McDonnell Douglas DC-9-31/32,
7 x DC-10-10, 16 x DC-10-30, 7 x MD-81, 58 x MD-82, 2 x MD-83.
On order: 18 x Boeing 737-500, 8 x 757-200, 12 x 767-300ER, 5 x 777-200B.
Continental Express operates 38 x ATR42, 3 x ATR72, 22 x Beech 1900,
32 x Embraer EMB-120.

by red and blue cheatlines enclosing a golden pencil line. The cheatlines are wrapped around the nose and rear fuselage. 'CHINA EASTERN' titles are applied on the mid-fuselage roof, in red Chinese characters and blue English wording. The tailfin is dominated by a red sun rising from a blue sea through which flies a white stylised bird at dawn.

Illustrated: Since taking delivery of its first Airbus A300-600R in November 1989, China Eastern has built up its fleet to 10 of the type.

a yellow tailfin and a stylised bird symbol enclosed in a circle, both in blue, and 'Condor' titles on the forward fuselage in matching blue Helvetica typeface. The aircraft body is in pristine white, with only the underside below wing level finished in pale grey.

Illustrated: Condor's McDonnell Douglas DC-10-30 trijet first entered service with the airline in November 1979 and is operated in a single-class Economy layout for 370 passengers.

Colour scheme: Continental's present livery was unveiled in February 1991. The scheme is based on blue, white and gold, with the blue tailfin the dominant feature incorporating a stylised three-dimensional globe in white latitudes and gold longitudes. A thin gold pinstripe divides the upper white fuselage from the grey belly. Simple blue 'Continental' titles are carried on the forward cabin roof.

Illustrated: Continental is one of the largest users of the McDonnell Douglas DC-10 trijet. The DC-10-30 is operated in a two-class layout seating 242 passengers and is used on all trans-Atlantic services.

CROATIA AIRLINES (OU/CTN)

Founded/First Service: 1989 as Zagreb Airlines, present name adopted in 1990
Base: Zagreb Pleso Airport, Zagreb, Croatia
Services: International passenger and cargo services from Zagreb to Amsterdam, Berlin, Brussels, Copenhagen, Dublin, Düsseldorf, Frankfurt, Istanbul, London, Moscow, Munich, Paris, Prague, Rome, Sarajevo, Skopje, Stockholm, Stuttgart, Tirana, Vienna and Zürich. Domestic flights link Zagreb with Brac, Dubrovnik, Mali Losinj, Osijek, Pula, Split and Zadar. Additional summer schedules and charters to serve local tourist industry.
Fleet (12): 3 x ATR42-300, 5 x Boeing 737-200A, 1 x Cessna 310R, 3 x Cessna 402C II.
On order: 6 x Airbus A319.
Colour scheme: Croatia Airlines' livery is built around the traditional red and white checked shield of the new national flag. It appears on the lower part of the tailfin in the form of an arrow flying above a light blue field extending to the base of the fin and along the full length of the fuselage underside. The only other displays on a clean white aircraft are 'CROATIA AIRLINES' titles in blue, the initial letter being 'speeded' along by a smaller red/white checked arrow.
Illustrated: Croatia Airlines operates the 42-seat ATR42-300 domestically and on some thinner European routes, backing up its
mainline fleet of ex-Lufthansa Boeing 737-200
Advanced twinjets.

CROSSAIR (LX/CRX)

Founded/First Service: 14 February 1975 as Business Flyers Basel AG, adopted present title 14 November 1978/2 July 1979
Base: EuroAirport Basel-Mulhouse-Freiburg, Basel, Switzerland
Services: Scheduled passenger services to 72 destinations in 14 European countries including some schedules for parent company Swissair. Also short-haul charter flights throughout Europe and to resort areas in North Africa and the Middle East.
Fleet (61): 4 x Avro RJ85, 12 x Avro RJ100, 8 x McDonnell Douglas MD-82/83, 15 x Saab 340B, 22 x Saab 2000.
On order: 17 x Saab 2000.
Colour scheme: Crossair's trademark, introduced in April 1993, consists of two painted patches, one on top of the other. The red Swiss rhomboid in the foreground is identical to that of parent company Swissair, while the blue area with an irregular outline behind, represents Europe, emphasised by the stars of the European Union. Along the side of the all white fuselage is a series of ingenious graphics, stretching from nose to tail. Two small separate patches of red and blue develop in phases towards the rear into a complete logo, denoting Switzerland's slow progress towards entry into the European Union, which Crossair hopes will eventually be achieved. The scheme conveys Crossair's closeness to Swissair, while at the same time illustrating its independence and commitment to Europe.
Illustrated: Crossair acquired eight McDonnell Douglas MD-80s when it took over Balair/CTA's short-haul charter operations in November 1995.

CSA CZECH AIRLINES (OK/CSA)

Founded/First Service: 19 July 1923/28 October 1923

Base: Ruzyne Airport, Prague, Czech Republic

Services: Operates to 57 international destinations, including extensive intra-European flights together with long-haul services to the Middle and Far East, and to North America. Points served from Prague are Abu Dhabi, Bangkok, Beirut, Dubai, Kuwait, Montreal, New York, Singapore, Tel Aviv and Toronto. Partnership with Continental Airlines connects Prague with a further 18 cities in the United States. Domestic services link Prague, Brno, Ostrava and Karlovy Vary, and there are also services to Bratislava, Piestany, Kosice, Tatry and Sliac in Slovakia.

Fleet (22): 2 x Airbus A310-300, 4 x ATR72-200, 2 x ATR42-300, 2 x Boeing 737-400, 8 x 737-500, 4 x Tupolev Tu-154M.

Colour scheme: The fresh white overall paint scheme is complemented by the red and blue colours, which make up the national flag. A full-length pencil-thin red cheatline above a broader blue line supports large red 'CSA' initials (standing for the Czech title of Ceské Aerolinie) and blue 'CZECH AIRLINES' lettering. The tailfin is dominated by a red/blue/red pendant flying from the leading edge, underscored by a thin red line.

Illustrated: The Airbus A310-300 was the first element in the airline's plans to gradually replace its ex-Soviet fleet, which now only retains the Tupolev Tu-154M. Both A310s entered service in Spring 1991.

CYPRUS AIRWAYS (CY/CYP)

Founded/First Service: 24 September 1947/6 October 1947
Base: Larnaca International Airport, Larnaca, Cyprus
Services: Scheduled international passenger services within Europe and the Middle East, linking Larnaca with Amman, Amsterdam, Athens, Bahrain, Beirut, Berlin, Birmingham, Brussels, Cairo, Damascus, Dubai, Frankfurt, Heraklion, Jeddah, Kuwait, Linz, London, Lyon, Manchester, Munich, Paris, Rhodes, Riyadh, Rome, Salzburg, Tel Aviv, Thessalonika, Vienna and Zürich. Some destinations are also served from Paphos. Charter flights through subsidiary, Eurocypria Airlines.
Fleet (12): 4 x Airbus A310-200, 8 x Airbus A320-200.
Colour scheme: The present livery introduced in late 1990 features twin 'straight through' cheatlines of royal blue and sunshine yellow below window level, separating the upper white from the lower grey fuselage. 'CYPRUS AIRWAYS' titles are promoted in blue on the mid-cabin roof. The tailfin displays the airline's white winged mountain goat symbol on a royal blue field, topped by two yellow bars and one blue.
Illustrated: Cyprus Airways was one of five launch customers for the Airbus A320. Of its fleet of eight aircraft, all powered by IAE V2500 turbofan engines, three are leased to Eurocypria Airlines for charter flights.

DELTA AIR LINES (DL/DAL)

Founded/First Service: 1924 as Huff Daland Dusters/17 June 1929. Became Delta Air Service in 1928 and Delta Air Lines in 1945

Base: Hartsfield International Airport, Atlanta, Georgia, United States

Services: Large passenger network serving 197 cities in 26 countries, including an extensive domestic feeder network operated by four commuter airlines under the 'Delta Connection' banner. Main hubs at Atlanta, Cincinnati, Dallas/Fort Worth, Los Angeles, New York, Orlando, Salt Lake City and Frankfurt. Intercontinental cities are Amsterdam, Athens, Barcelona, Berlin, Bombay, Brussels, Budapest, Bucharest, Copenhagen, Dublin, Frankfurt, Helsinki, Istanbul, Lisbon, London, Madrid, Munich, Nagoya, Paris, Prague, Rome, St Petersburg, Seoul, Stuttgart, Tokyo, Vienna, Warsaw and Zürich.

Fleet (539): 132 x Boeing 727-200A, 54 x 737-200A, 13 x 737-300, 86 x 757-200, 15 x 767-200, 26 x 767-300, 16 x 767-300ER, 31 x Lockheed L1011 TriStar 1, 1 x L1011 TriStar 200, 6 x L1011 TriStar 250, 17 x L1011 TriStar 500, 11 x McDonnell Douglas MD-11, 120 x MD-88, 11 x MD-90-30.

On order: 4 x Boeing 757-200, 7 x 767-300ER, 4 x McDonnell Douglas MD-11, 20 x MD90-30.

Colour scheme: Delta unveiled a new colour scheme in April 1997, representing the first major change in the company's livery for 35 years. Retaining the traditional colours of red, blue and white, it focuses on a blue windowline on a largely white fuselage widening at the front to include a red 'nosestrap' below. The blue/red theme is repeated on the engine cowlings, but reversed on the tailfin with a red flash on the leading edge ahead of the blue, with Delta reversed out in white. Delta Air Lines titles sit above the windowline, headed by the blue and red delta 'widget'.

Illustrated: A computer-generated image of Delta Air Lines revised livery.

EGYPTAIR (MS/MSR)

Founded/First Service: 7 June 1932 as Misrair/July 1933, present name adopted 10 October 1974
Base: Cairo International Airport, Heliopolis, Cairo, Egypt
Services: Passenger and cargo services throughout the Middle East and to the Far East, Africa, the United States and Europe. Flights outside Europe and the Middle East serve Abidjan, Accra, Bangkok, Bombay (Mumbai), Dar es Salaam, Entebbe, Johannesburg, Kano, Karachi, Lagos, Los Angeles, Manila, Nairobi, New York, Osaka, Sydney and Tokyo. Domestic flights link Cairo with 11 destinations.
Fleet (37): 9 x Airbus A300-600R, 5 x A300B4-200, 7 x A320-200, 3 x A340-200, 1 x Boeing 707-320C, 5 x 737-500, 2 x 747-300(SCD), 3 x 767-200ER, 2 x 767-300ER.
On order: 4 x Airbus A321-100, 1 x A340-200, 3 x Boeing 777-200.
Colour scheme: EgyptAir began modernising its corporate identity in early 1996. Retaining its ancient symbol of Horus, the falcon-headed solar god of Egyptian mythology, this is now depicted on a midnight blue tailfin in red and gold and repeated against the same blue background on the engine cowlings. 'EgyptAir' titles in blue forward are followed by Arabic script in red. The aircraft is otherwise painted in a fresh white.
Illustrated: EgyptAir has four A321-100s on order, further expanding its Airbus fleet.

EL AL ISRAEL AIRLINES (LY/ELY)

Founded/First Service: 15 November 1948/August 1949
Base: Ben Gurion International Airport, Tel Aviv, Israel
Services: Scheduled passenger and cargo services dominated by European connections and extending to the United States, Canada, Africa and the Far East. Intercontinental routes now serve Baltimore/Washington, Bangkok, Beijing, Bombay, Boston, Chicago, Hong Kong, Johannesburg, Los Angeles, Miami, Montreal, Nairobi, New Delhi, New York and Toronto. Wholly-owned subsidiary, Sun D'Or International Airlines, established on 1 October 1977, operates passenger charter flights to European resorts, using aircraft from the parent company.
Fleet (23): 2 x Boeing 737-200A, 5 x 747-200B, 2 x 747-200C, 1 x 747-200F, 3 x Boeing 747-400, 6 x 757-200, 4 x 767-200ER.
Colour scheme: The white fuselage is dissected by an unusual cheatline arrangement at window level, starting with bright blue and changing into a dark blue wedge in line with the wing leading edge. The upper rear fuselage continues the bright blue colouring across most of the tailfin which is crowned by the Israeli flag, dominated by the six-pointed Star of David. Prominent 'EL AL' titling in bright blue on the forward fuselage is interspersed with the Hebrew equivalent in dark blue.
Illustrated: The first Boeing 747-400 was delivered to El Al in May 1994 and has since been joined by two more. In El Al's configuration, the 747-400 seats 492 passengers in a three-class layout and is being used on routes to North America and London.

EMIRATES (EK/UAE)

Founded/First Service: May 1985/25 October 1985
Base: Dubai International Airport, Dubai, United Arab Emirates
Services: Scheduled passenger and cargo flights from Dubai to 38 destinations throughout the Middle East and to Europe and Asia, serving Abu Dhabi, Amman, Bandar Abbas, Bangkok, Beirut, Bombay (Mumbai), Cairo, Colombo, Comores, Damascus, Delhi, Dhaka, Dhahran, Doha, Frankfurt, Ho Chi Minh City, Hong Kong, Istanbul, Jakarta, Jeddah, Karachi, Kuwait, Larnaca, London Heathrow, Male, Manchester, Manila, Melbourne, Muscat, Nairobi, Nice, Paris, Riyadh, Rome, Shiraz, Singapore, Tehran and Zürich.
Fleet (19): 6 x Airbus A300-600R, 10 x A310-300, 3 x Boeing 777-200.
On order: 16 x Airbus A330-200, 4 x Boeing 777-200.
Colour scheme: A vast representation of the red, white and green United Arab Emirates flag flies upwards from the rear fuselage to cover most of the tail, providing the only flash of patriotic colours on the overall white fuselage. Gold 'Emirates' roof titling is displayed in English and Arabic, with the latter also appearing on the engine cowlings.
Illustrated: Emirates took delivery of its first Rolls-Royce Trent-powered Boeing 777-200 new-generation twinjet in summer 1996.

ESTONIAN AIR (OV/ELL)

Founded/First Service: 1 December 1991
Base: Tallinn-Ylemiste Airport, Tallinn, Estonia
Services: National flag services from Tallinn to Amsterdam, Copenhagen, Frankfurt, Hamburg, Helsinki, Kiev, London Gatwick, Minsk, Munich, Moscow, St Petersburg and Vilnius. No domestic services.
Fleet (16): 3 x Boeing 737-500, 7 x Tupolev Tu-134A (for sale), 2 x Tu-134A-3, 4 x Yakovlev Yak-40.
Colour scheme: Estonian Air uses the national colours of blue, black and white to good effect, although the black has been replaced by a deep shade of blue. Unusually, the upper part of the aircraft is in two-tone blue with the darker shade atop, while the lower half from below the windowline is finished in white. The light blue and white tailfin, divided by the company's stylised bird/arrow logo in dark blue, is an imaginative representation of the national

ETHIOPIAN AIRLINES (ET/ETH)

Founded/First Service: 26 December 1945/8 April 1946
Base: Bole International Airport, Addis Ababa, Ethiopia
Services: Flag services from Addis Ababa to points throughout Africa and to Abu Dhabi, Athens, Bangkok, Beijing, Bombay (Mumbai), Dubai, Frankfurt, Jeddah, Karachi, London, Muscat, Riyadh, Rome and Sana'. Also vital domestic flights to more than 40 destinations. All-cargo flights link Addis Ababa with Bombay (Mumbai), Dubai, Entebbe, Frankfurt, Jeddah, Johannesburg, Kinshasa, Luanda, Nairobi, New Delhi, Ostend and Rome.
Fleet (19): 2 x ATR42-300, 1 x Boeing 707-320C, 1 x 737-200, 4 x 757-200, 1 x 757-200PF, 2 x 767-200ER, 1 x DHC-5A Buffalo, 4 x DHC-6 Twin Otter 300, 5 x Fokker 50, 2 x Lockheed L100-30 Hercules.
Colour scheme: The livery is dominated by three attractive tail feathers in the national colours of green, yellow and red. These are complemented by a similarly coloured intricate cheatline which begins with a bright red lightning bolt at the cockpit windows and ends in a ribbon effect under the horizontal tailplane. The royal rampant lion has been retained on the forward fuselage.

EUROWINGS (EW/EWG)

Founded/First Service: 1 January 1993 from merger of NFD Luftverkehrs AG and RFG Regionalflug
Bases: Nuremberg and Dortmund Airports, Germany
Services: Scheduled regional passenger services within Germany and to other European nations. International destinations include Amsterdam, Brussels, Guernsey, Jersey, Krakow, London, Lyon, Newcastle, Nice, Olbia, Paris, Poznan, Prague, Vienna, Warsaw, Wroclaw and Zürich. Extensive domestic network serves 15 cities.
Fleet (32): 17 x ATR42-300, 6 x ATR72-200, 4 x ATR72-210, 5 x BAe 146-200.
On order: 3 x Airbus A319.
Colour scheme: Two speedwing arrows in red and blue, the latter with a curved contrail, form the principal element of the design, being applied on the white tailfin, engines and the forward fuselage. Black 'eurowings' titling is applied on the forward upper fuselage. A blue cheatline underscored by a thin pencil line in red,

flag. The engine cowlings are finished in dark blue and white with a light blue star. 'ESTONIAN AIR' titles below the forward windows are preceded by the airline symbol.

Illustrated: The Boeing 737-500, fitted out for 109 passengers in Club and Economy configuration, operates all main services to Western Europe.

Red 'ETHIOPIAN' lettering is displayed in English and Amharic, the official local language.

Illustrated: The Boeing extended-range 767-200ER flagship is operated on the airline's African services and on the main routes to London, Frankfurt and Bombay. They are fitted out for 196 passengers in a three-class configuration.

separates the white upper body from the grey underside of the aircraft. Small 'eurowings' titles break the blue cheatline at the rear, while the red pencil line is cut by the contrail of the logo.

Illustrated: Eurowings has ordered three Airbus A319 for charter flights to European and Mediterranean destinations.

EVA AIR (BR/EVA)

Founded/First Service: March 1989/1 July 1991
Base: Chiang Kai-Shek International Airport, Taipei, Taiwan
Services: Scheduled services to nearly 30 cities in Asia, Australia, New Zealand, Europe, the United States and Central America, including Anchorage, Auckland, Bangkok, Brisbane, Dubai, Fukuoka, Ho Chi Minh City, Hong Kong, Honolulu, Jakarta, Kuala Lumpur, London Gatwick, Los Angeles, Macau, Maldives, Manila, Melbourne, New York, Panama City, Penang, Phuket, San Francisco, Seattle, Seoul, Singapore, Sydney and Vienna. Domestic service between Taipei and Kaohsiung.
Fleet (27): 12 x Boeing 747-400, 4 x 767-200, 5 x 767-300ER, 6 x McDonnell Douglas MD-11. *On order:* 10 x McDonnell Douglas MD-90, 2 x MD-11F.
Colour scheme: The visual focal point of Evergreen's corporate identity is the aircraft tail which features a light green globe, displayed against a dark green background. The globe is positioned so that the upper left-hand corner is cut off at an angle, said to represent the new vistas of service innovation. The vital dynamism is further enhanced by the addition of a vertical strip of orange at the fin's outer edge, imparting a sense of hi-tech innovation. Dark green, the colour of durability, creates an image of stability and reliability. The words 'EVA AIR' are applied in light and dark green on the forward, all-white fuselage, under a thin orange line which stretches back all the way to the base of the fin.

Illustrated: Eva Air's first aircraft order was for the Boeing 767, which inaugurated the airline's first service in July 1991.

FEDEX (FEDERAL EXPRESS) (FM/FDX)

Founded/First Service: 1972/17 April 1973
Base: Memphis International Airport, Memphis, Tennessee, United States
Services: Scheduled air cargo and express freight delivery services now cover 325 airports in more than 200 countries across the globe from a Superhub at Memphis, regional hubs at Newark, Oakland and Fort Worth, metroplexes at Chicago and Los Angeles, and the Anchorage gateway. Major overseas facilities operated at London Stansted, Frankfurt, Paris, Subic Bay in the Philippines and in Japan.
Fleet (562): 18 x Airbus A300-600F, 28 x A310-200F, 75 x Boeing 727-100F/C, 88 x 727-200F Advanced, 2 x 747-100F, 10 x Cessna 208A Caravan I, 254 x 208B Caravan I Super Cargomaster, 24 x Fokker F27-500 Friendship, 8 x F27-600, 20 x McDonnell Douglas MD-11F, 13 x DC-10-10F, 22 x DC-10-30F.
On order: 18 x A300-600F, 9 x A310-200F, 36 x DC-10CF, 11 x MD-11F.
Colour scheme: Designed by Landor Associates, the 'FedEx' brand name is said to embrace speed, reliability, innovative technology and customer service. It is characterised by a bold sans serif typeface in dynamic shades of the purple and orange Federal Express colours, applied in large letters on the forward clean white fuselage, and in smaller size on the white engine cowlings and the all purple tailfin and rear fuselage. Embedded within the primary design is an arrow, symbolising the company's speed and efficiency.
Illustrated: FedEx operates a growing number of McDonnell Douglas MD-11F freighters, one seen positioning for take-off from Memphis International Airport.

FINNAIR (AY/FIN)

Founded/First Service: 1 November 1923/20 March 1924. Originally known as Aero OY, present name officially adopted in 1968, but used since 1953.

Base: Helsinki-Vantaa Airport, Helsinki, Finland

Services: Long-haul routes to Toronto, San Francisco, New York, Bangkok, Singapore, Beijing, Osaka and Tokyo, together with an extensive European network, serving 45 international destinations. The Beijing, Osaka and Tokyo routes are flown non-stop across Siberia. Finnair also flies to 21 local destinations in Finland. Charter traffic mainly to holiday resorts in the Mediterranean, the Canary Islands, South East Asia and the Caribbean. Subsidiaries Finnaviation and Karair have been integrated.

Fleet (51): 2 x Airbus A300B4-200, 6 x ATR72-200, 12 x McDonnell Douglas DC-9-51, 4 x MD-11, 17 x MD-82/83, 3 x MD-87, 7 x Saab 340A.

Colour scheme: The aircraft livery is a patriotic portrayal of the national colours of white and blue, symbolising snow and sky, and comprises a blue windowline which runs the full length of the fuselage, and a tail painted to represent the Finnish flag. Attention is drawn to the blue 'FINNAIR' titles with a smart sash in three shades of blue. A small company emblem, the flying 'F', is applied on the nose in white on a blue disk.

Illustrated: Finnair has always been a prolific user of McDonnell Douglas aircraft. In addition to its large short/medium-range twin-engined fleet, it also operates the MD-11 trijet on its long-haul routes.

GARUDA INDONESIA (GA/GIA)

Founded/First Service: 31 March 1950
Base: Soekarno-Hatta International Airport, Jakarta, Indonesia
Services: International scheduled passenger and cargo services to Abu Dhabi, Amsterdam, Auckland, Bangkok, Beijing, Brisbane, Cairns, Darwin, Dhahran, Frankfurt, Fukuoka, Guangzhou, Ho Chi Minh City, Hong Kong, Honolulu, Jeddah, Kuala Lumpur, London Gatwick, Los Angeles, Manila, Melbourne, Nagoya, Osaka, Paris, Riyadh, Rome, Seoul, Singapore, Sydney, Taipei, Tokyo and Zürich. Also extensive domestic network linking Jakarta and 30 other points throughout the Indonesian archipelago.
Fleet (58): 9 x Airbus A300B4-200, 10 x A300-600R, 4 x A330-300, 12 x Boeing 737-300, 6 x 747-200B, 5 x 747-400, 5 x McDonnell Douglas DC-10-30, 7 x MD-11. *On order:* 5 x Airbus A330-300, 5 x Boeing 747-400, 4 x 737-400, 2 x McDonnell Douglas MD-11.
Colour scheme: One of the smartest airline liveries, it was designed by Landor Associates of San Francisco and unveiled in September 1985. Its centre-piece is a modern representation of the 'Garuda', the sacred bird of Hinduism, which is displayed on the deep-blue fin in progressive shades from blue to turquoise. The five wing feathers symbolise the five national ideals. The Garuda also appears alongside dark blue 'Garuda Indonesia' titling on the all-white fuselage. The national flag is painted above the first cabin windows.

Illustrated: Garuda Indonesia's fleet is headed by Airbus twins, including the A300-600R of which 10 are operated.

GHANA AIRWAYS (GH/GHA)

Founded/First Service: 4 July 1958/16 July 1958
Base: Kotoka International Airport, Accra, Ghana
Services: International passenger and cargo services to Europe and the United States, serving Düsseldorf, London, Rome and New York, and regionally from Accra to Abidjan, Banjul, Conakry, Cotonou, Dakar, Freetown, Harare, Johannesburg, Lagos and Lomé.
Fleet (3): 1 x McDonnell Douglas DC-9-51, 2 x DC-10-30.
Colour scheme: Based on the national tricolour, the aircraft is distinguished by a broad cheatline in red, yellow and green which widens at the base of the tail. The company insignia, comprising a black star, the symbol of African freedom, and red, yellow and green wings, is carried on the white centre engine of the DC-10, surmounted by a large national flag. The pan-African colours of the flag stand for revolution (red), the country's natural resources (yellow), and agriculture (green). Black 'GHANA AIRWAYS' titles are displayed on the mid-upper fuselage.
Illustrated: Ghana Airways took delivery of its first McDonnell Douglas DC-10-30 in February 1983. The type remains the only long-haul aircraft in its fleet and operates the intercontinental routes to Europe and North America, together with its prime inter-African route to Johannesburg. It is operated in a two-class configuration with 34 Premier and 238 Economy Class seats.

GULF AIR (GF/GFA)

Founded/First Service: 24 March 1950/5 July 1950
Base: Muharraq International Airport, Bahrain
Services: Intercontinental route network of 50 destinations in 39 countries, extending from the Middle East into Europe, East Africa, the Indian sub-continent, the Far East and Australasia. In addition to many points in the Middle East, the route system includes Amsterdam, Athens, Bangkok, Bombay (Mumbai), Casablanca, Colombo, Dar es Salaam, Delhi, Dhaka, Entebbe, Frankfurt, Hong Kong, Istanbul, Jakarta, Johannesburg, Karachi, Khartoum, Larnaca, London, Madras, Manila, Melbourne, Nairobi, Paris, Rome, Singapore, Sydney, Trivandrum and Zürich.
Fleet (37): 14 x Airbus A320-200, 5 x A340-300, 18 x 767-300ER.
On order: 6 x A330-300, 1 x A340-300.
Colour scheme: The livery features the national colours of the four states, Bahrain, Qatar, Oman and the United Arab Emirates. A maroon, green and red 'chin' flash leads the all-white fuselage, above which appear English and Arabic 'GULF AIR' titles in gold lettering. Vertical maroon, green and red bands, separated by thin white stripes, also colour the top half of the tail, below which flies a golden falcon, symbolic of the Arabian peninsula.
Illustrated: Gulf Air became the first airline in the Middle East to take delivery of the four-engined Airbus A340-300 in May 1994. A total of six have been ordered with CFM International CFM56-5C2 turbofans.

IBERIA (IB/IBE)

Founded/First Service: 7 July 1940

Base: Barajas Airport, Madrid, Spain

Services: International flag services to all major European destinations, the Americas, North and West Africa, Middle East and Japan. Particularly strong in Latin America, serving Asunçion, Bogotá, Buenos Aires, Caracas, Cancun, Guatemala City, Havana, Lima, Managua, Mexico City, Montevideo, Panama City, Quito, Rio de Janeiro, Santiago de Chile, Santo Domingo, San José, San Juan, San Salvador, San Pedro Sula and São Paulo, some via its Miami hub. Also extensive domestic scheduled and European leisure flights mainly through a number of subsidiary companies, including Aviaco, Binter and Viva Air.

Fleet (111): 6 x Airbus A300B4-100/200, 22 x A320-200, 4 x A340-300, 28 x Boeing 727-200A, 7 x 747-200B(SCD), 8 x 757-200, 2 x McDonnell Douglas DC-8-62F, 1 x DC-8-71F, 5 x DC-10-30, 4 x DC-9-32, 24 x MD-87.

On order: 4 x Airbus A340-200, 8 x Boeing 757-200.

Colour scheme: A bright sunshine livery successfully combines the red and gold colours of the national flag with an allusion to the country's holiday attraction. Triple cheatlines of red, orange and gold sweep down from behind the cockpit and along the fuselage at and above the windowline. White italic 'IBERIA' titles are set into the red and orange of the cheatline. A quartered 'IB' logo in red and gold on the white tail carries a royal crown.

Illustrated: Iberia uses a large fleet of the shortest version of the McDonnell Douglas MD-80 twinjet series, the MD-87.

ICELANDAIR (FI/ICE)

Founded/First Service: 3 June 1937/4 May 1938
Bases: Reykjavik and Keflavik Airports, Iceland
Services: International scheduled services to 22 destinations including Amsterdam, Baltimore/Washington, Barcelona, Copenhagen, Faroe Islands, Frankfurt, Fort Lauderdale, Glasgow, Hamburg, London, Luxembourg, Milan, Narssarssuaq, New York, Orlando, Oslo, Paris, Reykjavik (Keflavik), Stockholm, Vienna, Washington and Zürich. Domestic flights link 10 points with the capital Reykjavik. Charters to Greenland and the Mediterranean.
Fleet (11): 4 x Boeing 737-400, 3 x 757-200ER, 4 x Fokker 50.
Colour scheme: The scheme displays the traditional Icelandic colours of white and blue in a striking, yet simple fashion. A conventional 'straight through' windowline in mid-blue is trimmed by a similarly-coloured pinstripe below and contrasted by black 'ICELANDAIR' lettering above. A small Icelandic flag appears on the forward fuselage. The company's symbol, a heavily stylised, flowing 'F', standing for Flugleidr, its Icelandic name, adorns the white tail.
Illustrated: Icelandair operates one of the youngest fleets in Europe, including the Boeing 757-200, which operates trans-Atlantic flights to the United States.

IRAN AIR (IR/IRA)

Founded/First Service: February 1962
Base: Mehrabad Airport, Tehran, Islamic Republic of Iran
Services: Scheduled passenger and cargo services within the Middle East, and to the Asian CIS republics, the Far East and Europe. International destinations include Abu Dhabi, Almaty, Amsterdam, Ashkabad, Athens, Bahrain, Baku, Beijing, Bombay, Damascus, Doha, Dubai, Frankfurt, Geneva, Hamburg, Istanbul, Jeddah, Karachi, Kuala Lumpur, Kuwait, Larnaca, London, Madrid, Muscat, Paris, Rome, Sharjah, Tashkent, Tokyo and Vienna. A domestic passenger network linking 20 towns and cities is also operated.
Fleet (35): 5 x Airbus A300B2-200, 2 x A300-600R, 4 x Boeing 707-320C, 2 x 727-100, 5 x 727-200A, 3 x 737-200A, 1 x 747-100, 2 x 747-200B (SCD), 1 x 747-200F, 4 x 747SP, 6 x Fokker 100.
Colour scheme: Iran Air has modernised its livery, principally by removing the cheatlines. The aircraft are now predominantly white, giving way to a grey underside at wing level. A thin deep blue line sweeps up the leading edge of the tailfin and flows round to fill the upper third above the Homa, a mythical bird of ancient Persia, symbolising good fortune and great strength, which is the traditional symbol of Iran Air. 'IRAN AIR' titles are carried on the forward cabin roof, ahead of the national flag and small 'The Airline of the Islamic Republic of Iran' wording. Arabic titles appear at the rear.

Illustrated: Iran Air continues to use the Boeing 747SP on its longer routes.
Chris Doggett/F. Stop International

JAPAN AIRLINES — JAL (JL/JAL)

Founded/First Service: 1 August 1951/25 October 1951
Bases: Narita Airport, Tokyo and Kansai International Airport, Osaka, Japan
Services: International passenger and cargo services worldwide, except to Africa, together with high-density, high-frequency domestic flights linking Tokyo with 14 major Japanese cities. European destinations are Amsterdam, Berlin, Düsseldorf, Frankfurt, London, Madrid, Milan, Moscow, Paris, Rome and Zürich.
Fleet (128): 2 x Boeing 737-400, 6 x 747-100LR/SR/SUD, 29 x 747-200B/F, 13 x 747-300, 24 x 747-400, 8 x 747-400D, 3 x 767-200, 17 x 767-300, 3 x 777-200, 14 x McDonnell Douglas DC-10-40, 9 x MD-11. *On order:* 2 x Boeing 737-400, 18 x 747-400, 2 x 767-300, 7 x 777-200, 5 x 777-300, 1 x McDonnell Douglas MD-11.
Colour scheme: The present design, developed by Landor Associates of San Francisco, features a fusion of the JAL letters with a red square and grey band. JAL's 'Tsuru', a stylised version of a traditional family crest using the crane, an auspicious bird in Japan, dominates the tail of the aircraft. The straight standing black 'JAL' letters are designed to express dedication and reliability. The red square symbolises the further strengthening of the JAL corporation, with the burning enthusiasm of youth and energy. The grey band indicates a sense of vibrancy and the spirited stance taken in meeting future challenges.
Illustrated: Japan Airlines is the largest Boeing 747 operator. When the last 747-400 is delivered in the year 2000, its fleet will total almost 100 aircraft.

JAL

JAT YUGOSLAV AIRLINES (JU/JAT)

Founded/First Service: 1 April 1947
Base: Belgrade International Airport, Belgrade, Federal Republic of Yugoslavia
Services: Flag services linking the capital Belgrade with destinations in Europe, North America, Australia and the Middle and Far East. Cities served include Amman, Amsterdam, Athens, Beirut, Cairo, Chicago/O'Hare, Copenhagen, Dubai, Düsseldorf, Frankfurt, Kiev, Larnaca, London, Malta, Melbourne, Montreal, Moscow, New York, Paris, Rome, Singapore, Stockholm, Stuttgart, Sydney, Tel Aviv, Thessalonika, Timisoara, Toronto, Vienna and Zürich. Some routes still subject to approval by respective Governments.
Fleet (28): 3 x ATR72-200, 6 x Boeing 727-200A, 9 x 737-300, 9 x McDonnell Douglas DC-9-32, 1 x DC-10-30.
Colour scheme: The present attractive livery of JAT was introduced when it resumed services in October 1994, following its grounding two years earlier after the introduction of UN sanctions. Highlight of the all-white fuselage are the blue, white and red flame markings on the tailfin, alluding to the national flag and coat of arms. Bold blue 'JAT' initials are followed by the airline's full name 'Jugoslovenski Aerotransport' on the starboard side, and in English on the port side of the aircraft.
Illustrated: Flag carrier JAT has been using the Boeing 737-300 on its main European routes since July 1985. *Terry Shone*

KENYA AIRWAYS (KQ/KQA)

Founded/First Service: 22 January 1977/4 February 1977
Bases: Jomo Kenyatta International Airport (Embakasi), Nairobi and Moi International Airport, Mombasa, Kenya
Services: Scheduled passenger services from Nairobi and Mombasa to 23 regional and intercontinental destinations in Africa, Europe, the Middle East and Indian subcontinent. Points served include Addis Ababa, Bombay (Mumbai), Bujumbura, Cairo, Copenhagen, Dar es Salaam, Dubai, Entebbe, Frankfurt, Harare, Jeddah, Johannesburg, Karachi, Khartoum, Lilongwe, London Heathrow, Lusaka, Paris Orly, Rome, Seychelles, Stockholm, Zanzibar and Zürich. Domestic routes serve Kisumu, Mombasa, Malindi and Nairobi.
Fleet (8): 3 x Airbus A310-300, 2 x Boeing 737-200A, 3 x Fokker 50.
On order: 2 x Boeing 737-300.
Colour scheme: A triple cheatline in the national colours of black, red and green runs along the fuselage below the windows and extends the whole length of the fuselage. Black 'Kenya Airways' titles are carried on the white cabin roof, together with the Kenyan flag, whose colours are separated by white which stands for peace, and includes a Masai shield and two spears, symbolising the defence of freedom. Stylised, interlinked 'KA' initials are painted on the tail in red within a black circle.
Illustrated: Flagship of the Kenya Airways fleet is the Airbus A310, which serves all European cities on the scheduled network.

KLM ROYAL DUTCH AIRLINES (KL/KLM)

Founded/First Service: 7 October 1919/17 May 1920
Base: Schiphol Airport, Amsterdam, The Netherlands
Services: International passenger and cargo services to more than 150 cities in 83 countries on all continents, including all major points in Europe. Subsidiary KLM Cityhopper provides a link between key European cities and Amsterdam, from where connections are available for onward flights with KLM and its partner airlines, particularly Northwest Airlines and Air UK.
Fleet (104): 15 x Boeing 737-300, 16 x 737-400, 3 x 747-300, 10 x 747-300 Combi, 5 x 747-400, 11 x 747-400 Combi, 6 x 767-300, 6 x Fokker 100, 8 x McDonnell Douglas MD-11. *KLM Cityhopper:* 10 x Fokker 50, 3 x Fokker 70, 11 x Saab 340B. *On order:* 4 x Boeing 767-300.
Colour scheme: A deep blue windowline is flanked by a narrower white stripe below and a light blue cabin roof. The 'KLM' logotype (from the Dutch name Koninklijke Luchtvaart Maatschappij), topped by a royal crown, is painted in light blue on the all white tailfin. The logo also appears in all white on the cabin roof. The name of each aircraft is set forward in the lower white fuselage stripe.
Illustrated: KLM Royal Dutch Airlines was the first European carrier to operate the Boeing 747-400, taking delivery of the first aircraft in May 1989.

KOREAN AIR (KE/KAL)

Founded/First Service: June 1962
Base: Kimpo International Airport, Seoul, Korea
Services: Extensive schedule of international services to many regional destinations and to Europe, North and South America, the Middle East, Africa, Australia and New Zealand. European destinations from Seoul are Amsterdam, Frankfurt, London, Madrid, Moscow, Paris, Rome and Zürich, while Anchorage, Atlanta, Boston, Chicago, Dallas, Los Angeles, New York/Newark, Toronto, Vancouver and Washington DC are points served in North America. Also dense domestic network.
Fleet (97): 5 x Airbus A300-600, 18 x A300-600R, 8 x A300B4-200, 2 x A300F4-200, 4 x Boeing 747-200B, 1 x 747-200C, 10 x 747-200F, 3 x 747-300C, 19 x 747-400, 2 x 747SP, 12 x Fokker 100, 5 x McDonnell Douglas MD-11, 6 x MD-82, 2 x MD-83.
On order: 7 x Airbus A330-300, 10 x Boeing 747-400, 4 x 747-400F, 4 x 777-200, 8 x 777-300, 2 x McDonnell Douglas MD-83.
Colour scheme: A pale shade of sky blue colours the entire upper fuselage and tail unit, below which runs a silver cheatline, representing the sea. The company logo, known as the 'Taeguk', combines the red yin and blue yang symbols representing the opposing forces of nature, in this case heaven and earth, with white added to show 'endless strength of progress'. It is promoted on the tailfin and in place of the letter 'O' in the 'KOREAN AIR' fuselage titling. This striking livery was introduced in 1984.
Illustrated: Korean Air has a large fleet of Boeing 747-400s and more on order.

KUWAIT AIRWAYS (KU/KAC)

Founded/First Service: March 1954/April 1954

Base: Kuwait International Airport, Kuwait

Services: Predominantly Middle East and European network, with some extensions to the United States and the Far East. Destinations outside the Middle East include Amsterdam, Athens, Bangkok, Bombay (Mumbai), Chicago, Colombo, Copenhagen, Dhaka, Frankfurt, Geneva, Istanbul, Jakarta, Karachi, Larnaca, London, Madrid, Manila, New Delhi, New York, Paris, Rome and Singapore.

Fleet (24): 1 x Airbus A300C4-600, 6 x A300-600R, 4 x A310-300, 3 x A320-200, 4 x A340-200, 2 x Boeing 747-200B(SCD), 1 x 747-400 Combi, 3 x G-1159 Gulfstream IV.

On order: 2 x Boeing 777-200.

Colour scheme: A broad cheatline below the windows in ocean blue, edged on top in black and underscored by a darker blue line, provides a continuous band around the clean white fuselage. The company's black bird symbol flies reversed out in white on the largely blue tail, like the cheatline trimmed in black and darker blue. 'KUWAIT AIRWAYS' titles are applied in blue on the cabin roof, in both English and Arabic, and are repeated at the base of the tailfin in English only. The national flag, whose colours of green, white, red and black reflect Kuwait's membership of the Arab world, appears on the very top of the tail.

Illustrated: Kuwait Airways has re-equipped its fleet largely with Airbus aircraft, including the latest four-engined A340-200s, all delivered in the first half of 1995.

LAUDA AIR (NG/LDA)

Founded/First Service: 24 May 1979
Base: Schwechat Airport, Vienna, Austria
Services: Scheduled European services from Barcelona, Berlin, Brussels, Düsseldorf, Frankfurt, Lisbon, London, Madrid, Manchester, Milan, Munich, Nice and Rome, feeding into its long-haul flights out of Vienna and Salzburg. These serve Miami in the United States; Bangkok, Ho Chi Minh City, Hong Kong, Phuket and Singapore in the Far East; and Sydney and Melbourne in Australia. Winter schedule includes Colombo and Malé.
Fleet (19): 2 x Boeing 737-300, 2 x 737-400, 5 x 767-300ER, 7 x Canadair CL-65-100ER Regional Jet, 1 x Cessna Citation II, 1 x Dassault Falcon 20, 1 x Learjet 60.
On order: 2 x Boeing 737-800, 4 x 777-200.
Colour scheme: Lauda Air's visual identity was revised in October 1996, to provide unobtrusive elegance, optical grace and lightness. Developed by the airline's creative director Hannes Rausch, it is dominated by a large red 'double L' motif, now with a discreet golden outline, which covers the fin and alludes to the Austrian national flag. The 'double L' is repeated as the first letter in similarly bright red 'Lauda' roof titling. The angel motif with the words 'Service is our Success', has been changed to shimmering gold and is applied behind the airline name and on the tail assembly. The upper fuselage is now a mellow light grey, and a gold waterline provides separation from the dark grey underside, which is cut off at the rear in line with the leading edge of the tail logo.

Illustrated: Lauda Air uses its Boeing 767-300ER on all long-haul services to America, the Far East and Australia.

LITHUANIAN AIRLINES (TE/LIL)

Founded/First Service: 1991

Base: Vilnius International Airport, Vilnius, Lithuania

Services: International and regional services to points in the CIS and Europe from Vilnius to Amsterdam, Berlin, Copenhagen, Dublin, Ekaterinburg, Frankfurt, Istanbul, Kiev, Larnaca, London Heathrow, Mineraly Vody, Moscow, Odessa, Paris, Rome, St Petersburg, Samara, Stockholm, Tashkent, Ufa and Warsaw. Frankfurt and Moscow also served from Palanga. Regular charters to Casablanca, Damascus and Tel Aviv.

Fleet (16): 3 x Boeing 737-200, 1 x Lockheed L-1329 JetStar, 2 x Saab 340A, 1 x Tupolev Tu-134, 2 x Tu-134A-3, 2 x Yakovlev Yak-42, 5 x Yak-42D.

Colour scheme: The largely white aircraft have a bright red underside, with the colour sweeping up at the rear to form a red tailfin. A broad grey shadowline under the windows widens at the rear, stopping short of the tail. Two white letters 'L' form a bird symbol flying in a white circle. Red italic 'Lithuanian Airlines' titles are applied on the upper fuselage, preceded by the national flag of red, blue and yellow.

Illustrated: Although main services are now flown by the Boeing 737, the airline retains some ex-Soviet aircraft including the Yak-42D trijet, operated in a 120-seat configuration. *Terry Shone*

LOT POLISH AIRLINES (LO/LOT)

Founded/First Service: 1 January 1929
Base: Okęcie Airport, Warsaw, Poland
Services: Widespread European network extending to the Middle East and North Africa, in addition to long-haul services reaching eastwards to Bangkok and Beijing, and across the North Atlantic to Chicago, Montreal, New York (J. F. Kennedy International and Newark) and Toronto. A comprehensive domestic route system serves Warsaw, Krakow, Katowice, Rzeszow, Wroclaw, Poznan, Szczecin and Gdansk.
Fleet (23): 8 x ATR72-200, 5 x Boeing 737-400, 6 x 737-500, 2 x Boeing 767-200ER, 2 x 767-300ER.
On order: 2 x Boeing 737-800.
Colour scheme: The aircraft livery on an all white fuselage is centred on a large blue 'LOT' fuselage logo (LOT means flight), which is followed by a solid cheatline, lining up with the top of the lettering. The blue fin contains the Polish flag behind the historic flying crane insignia in a white circle, first introduced in 1929. The airline name appears in English on the port side and in Polish (Polskie Linie Lotnicze) on the starboard side. A blue flash of colour also extends from behind the nose to the underside of the cockpit windows.
Illustrated: The ATR72-200 took over domestic services from the Antonov An-24 from 1991. It is also used on thinner regional flights.

LTU INTERNATIONAL AIRWAYS (LT/LTU)

Founded/First Service: 20 October 1955/spring 1956
Registered name Lufttransport-Unternehmen
Base: Düsseldorf-Rhein/Ruhr Airport, Düsseldorf, Germany
Services: Scheduled European and international leisure flights, supplemented by charters, operated from all main German airports. Long-haul destinations include Abu Dhabi, Acapulco, Bangkok, Barbados, Cancun, Cape Town, Cayo Largo, Colombo, Curaçao, Denpasar/Bali, Durban, Fort Myers, Havana, Los Angeles, Malé, Miami, Montego Bay, Orlando, Phuket, Puerto Plata, Punta Cana, San José, Santo Domingo, Santa Cruz, Tampa, Varadero and Windhoek. Wholly-owned division LTU Süd International, based in Munich, and LTE International, based at Palma de Mallorca.
Fleet (27): 6 x Airbus A330-300, 12 x Boeing 757-200, 5 x 767-300ER, 4 x McDonnell Douglas MD-11.
Colour scheme: A bright red aircraft roof extends to fill the tailfin, which incorporates a white 'LTU' logo, repeated in red behind the cockpit windows. A red cheatline separates a white windowline and natural metal finish below. Engine cowlings are painted white.
Illustrated: LTU is the only German operator of the 335-seat twin-engined Airbus A330-300.

LUFTHANSA GERMAN AIRLINES (LH/DLH)

Founded/First Service: 6 January 1926

Base: Frankfurt-Rhein/Main Airport, Frankfurt, Germany

Services: Extensive worldwide system of scheduled passenger and cargo services, linking Germany with 227 destinations in 88 countries throughout Europe, and in Africa, the Middle and Far East, Australasia, North America, Central America and South America. Some domestic and thinner European routes supporting aircraft of less than 100-seat capacity, flown by subsidiary, Lufthansa CityLine, formerly DLT.

Fleet (229): 11 x Airbus A300-600, 2 x A300-600R, 12 x A310-300, 8 x A319-100, 33 x A320-200, 15 x A321-100, 6 x A340-200, 7 x A340-300, 22 x Boeing 737-200A, 43 x 737-300, 7 x 737-300QC, 6 x 737-400, 30 x 737-500, 4 x 747-200B, 4 x 747-200B(SCD), 12 x 747-400, 7 x 747-400(SCD).

Lufthansa CityLine: 15 x Avro RJ85, 30 x Canadair CL-65-100 Regional Jet, 12 x Fokker 50. *Lufthansa Cargo Airline:* 2 x Boeing 737-200F, 1 x 737-300F, 10 x 747-200F, 5 x McDonnell Douglas DC-8-73F.

On order: 12 x Airbus A319-100, 5 x A321-100, 5 x A340-300, 3 x Boeing 747-400.

Colour scheme: Centrepoint of the aircraft livery is the 'flying crane' symbol, which goes back to the earliest days of German aviation when it was carried by Deutscher Aero Lloyd. It is most prominently displayed in a yellow disk within a thin blue circle on the dark blue tail, and also appears under the cockpit in blue outline. Similarly coloured 'Lufthansa' titles in Helvetica script appear on the fuselage which is coloured white from the wingline upwards, and light grey below.

Illustrated: Lufthansa's Boeing 747-400s are configured for 387 passengers.

LUXAIR (LG/LGL)

Founded/First Service: 1961/April 1962
Base: Findel Airport, Luxembourg
Services: Scheduled passenger services within Europe only, linking Luxembourg with Alicante, Arrecife, Athens, Barcelona, Bastia, Berlin, Copenhagen, Faro, Frankfurt, Fuerteventura, Geneva, Hamburg, Ibiza, Larnaca, Las Palmas de Gran Canaria, Lisbon, London Heathrow and Stansted, Madrid, Malaga, Manchester, Milan/Bergamo, Munich, Naples, Nice, Oporto, Palma, Paris, Prague, Rimini, Rome, Saarbrücken, Salzburg, Strasbourg, Tenerife, Turin, Venice and Vienna. Direct flights are also operated from neighbouring airports in France and Germany. Feeder services under the title of Luxair Commuter. Luxairtours provides charter flights to the Mediterranean, the Atlantic Coast and the Canary Islands.
Fleet (10): 2 x Boeing 737-400, 4 x 737-500, 4 x Fokker 50.
Luxair Commuter: 3 x Embraer EMB-120RT Brasilia.
Colour scheme: Pale blue and white are the dominant colours of the Luxair livery, with a broad blue windowline separating the upper white and lower grey fuselage and the blue tail promoting the company emblem in white. This consists of a stylised L-shaped arrow enclosed in an outline circle. Strong black 'LUXAIR' titling in capital letters painted on the cabin roof behind the forward passenger door. The national and European Union flags are carried on mid-fuselage. Names of princes and *châteaux*, together with their respective coats of arms, are carried on the nose of the aircraft.
Illustrated: Europe's smallest flag carrier uses a small fleet of Boeing 737s to serve the main routes on its intra-European network. *Terry Shone*

MAERSK AIR (DM/DMA)

Founded/First Service: January 1970
Base: Copenhagen Airport, Dragoer, Denmark
Services: Regional European schedules from Copenhagen and Billund to London (Gatwick) and from Billund to Amsterdam, Brussels, Frankfurt, Paris and Stockholm. Domestic flights serve Odense, Esbjerg, Billund, Vojens, Bornholm, and Vagar in the Faroe Islands. Under the title of 'Maersk Helicopters' also undertakes helicopter flights from Esbjerg, while subsidiary Star Air operates contract cargo schedules mostly for UPS with five Boeing 727-100s.
Fleet (43): 3 x Eurocopter AS332L Super Puma, 2 x SA 365N Dauphin II,
1 x BAe 125-700B, 2 x Bell 212, 16 x Boeing 737-300, 4 x 737-500, 6 x 757-500SP,
9 x Fokker 50.
On order: 12 x 737-700.
Colour scheme: The aircraft livery employs an overall base colour of light blue with twin cheatlines below the windows in medium and dark blue trimmed in white. The seven-pointed star company logo is promoted in white within a white outline box, both on the tail and the forward fuselage in front of 'MAERSK' titles.
Illustrated: The Maersk Air twin-engined fleet is headed by the Boeing 737-300 which first entered service with the airline in summer 1985.

MALAYSIA AIRLINES (MH/MAS)

Founded/First Service: April 1971/9 June 1971

Base: Subang International Airport, Kuala Lumpur, Malaysia

Services: Extensive domestic and regional services, as well as long-haul routes to Australasia, the Middle East, Europe and the Americas, serving total of 76 international points. Intercontinental destinations include Adelaide, Amman, Amsterdam, Auckland, Beijing, Brisbane, Buenos Aires, Brussels, Cairns, Cape Town, Christchurch, Darwin, Dubai, Frankfurt, Istanbul, Jeddah, Johannesburg, London, Los Angeles, Madrid, Mauritius, Melbourne, Mexico City, Paris, Perth, Rome, San Francisco, Sydney, Tehran, Tokyo, Vienna and Zürich.

Fleet (107): 1 x Airbus A300B4-200, 12 x A330-300, 2 x 737-300F, 41 x 737-400, 9 x 737-500, 2 x 747-200B, 1 x 747-300(SCD), 13 x 747-400C, 6 x DHC-6 Twin Otter 300, 11 x Fokker 50, 4 x McDonnell Douglas DC-10-30, 3 x MD-11, 2 x MD-11F.
On order: 10 x Boeing 747-400, 11 x 777-200, 4 x 777-300.

Colour scheme: The modern livery is highlighted by the fresh white upper fuselage carrying red and mid-blue cheatlines with a trailing sweep at the rear to accentuate design symmetry and balance. The corporate image in red and blue, dividing equally at mid-spine, dominates the tailfin. It retains the essence of the Kelantan *Wau Bulan*, or Moon Dragon kite, while achieving a more aerodynamic posture. Predominantly blue 'malaysia' titles appear on the forward cabin roof preceded by the national flag. The letters 'm', 'a' and 's' bear red clippings to denote the initials of the airline's full name.

Illustrated: Malaysia's long-haul fleet comprises three versions of the Boeing 747, including this 747-300 Combi.

MALÉV HUNGARIAN AIRLINES (MA/MAH)

Founded/First Service: 26 April 1946 as Maszovlet, present name 25 November 1954

Base: Ferihegy Airport, Budapest, Hungary

Services: Inter-European and Near East network serving most capital cities and other major industrial and business centres, as well as long-haul routes to the United States and Thailand. Services extend from Budapest to Amsterdam, Athens, Atlanta, Bangkok, Barcelona, Beirut, Berlin, Brussels, Bucharest, Cairo, Cologne, Copenhagen, Damascus, Düsseldorf, Frankfurt, Hamburg, Helsinki, Istanbul, Kiev, Larnaca, London, Madrid, Milan, Moscow, Munich, New York, Paris, Prague, Rome, Sofia, St Petersburg, Stockholm, Stuttgart, Tel Aviv, Thessalonika, Tirana, Varna, Venice, Vienna, Warsaw and Zürich.

Fleet (27): 6 x Boeing 737-200A, 4 x 737-300, 2 x 737-400, 2 x 767-200ER, 3 x Fokker 70, 3 x Tupolev Tu-134A-3, 7 x Tu-154B-2.

Colour scheme: The latest livery features a sweep of blue at the rear of the clean overall white fuselage and the tail, which carries fin flashes in the national colours of red, white and green, going back to the earliest days of Hungary's history. Blue 'MALEV' titles appear on the forward cabin roof, alongside the flag and additional smaller 'Hungarian Airlines' lettering. The nose cone is also painted blue.

Illustrated: Malév's rapidly diminishing ex-Soviet fleet still includes the three-engined Tupolev Tu-154B-2. *Peter Zsille*

MARTINAIR HOLLAND (MP/MPH)

Founded/First Service: 24 May 1958 as Martin's Air Charter, present title adopted April 1968
Base: Schiphol Airport, Amsterdam, The Netherlands
Services: Worldwide cargo charter flights, principally over the Europe-Far East 'corridor' via the Middle East, and to Australia, Mexico, Africa, South America and the United States. Passenger inclusive-tour services from Amsterdam serving a number of destinations in Europe, Mexico, Canada and Thailand, and scheduled services across the North Atlantic to the United States, the Dominican Republic, Jamaica, Cuba, Puerto Rico and Barbados.
Fleet (18): 2 x Boeing 747-200C, 1 x 747-200F, 6 x 767-300ER,
2 x Cessna 650 Citation VI, 1 x Dornier Do228-200 (operated on behalf of the Department of Public Works), 5 x McDonnell Douglas MD-11CF, 1 x MD-11F.
Colour scheme: A warm red windowline runs the full length of the fuselage, terminating at an angle just short of the horizontal tailplane. A stylised red 'M', shaped into an arrow, dominates the white fin. Black 'Martinair' titles are displayed on the upper fuselage.
Illustrated: Martinair utilises its Boeing 767-300s on passenger flights, fitted out for 24 Club and 248 Economy Class passengers.

MERIDIANA (IG/ISS)

Founded/First Service: 24 March 1963 as Alisarda, present name adpted September 1991

Base: Costa Smeralda Airport, Olbia, Sardinia, Italy

Services: Scheduled domestic passenger flights and cross-border services to 10 destinations in six European countries, including seasonal routes from Sardinia. Apart from domestic services, Meridiana links London from Florence and Verona. Points on the network are Amsterdam, Barcelona, Bergamo, Bologna, Cagliari, Catania, Florence, Frankfurt, Geneva, Genoa, London, Milan, Munich, Naples, Nice, Palermo, Paris, Pisa, Rome, Turin, Venice, Verona and Zürich.

Fleet (18): 1 x Bell 412, 4 x British Aerospace 146-200, 5 x Douglas DC-9-51, 8 x McDonnell Douglas MD-82.

Colour scheme: The colour scheme is dominated by a white circle on a predominantly warm red tailfin, incorporating the company insignia composed of meridians — imaginary lines joining the North and South Poles at right angles to the Equator. The base of the fin is supported by a thin yellow and broader purple line. A similar yellow cheatline is sandwiched between red and purple lines extending the full length of the fuselage below the windows. Black 'Meridiana' titles appear forward ahead of the wing. The 146 carries the company symbol on the outer engines.

Illustrated: Flagship of the Meridiana fleet is the McDonnell Douglas MD-82, which is operated in a 165-seat configuration.

MIDDLE EAST AIRLINES MEA (ME/MEA)

Founded/First Service: May 1945/1 January 1946
Base: Beirut International Airport, Beirut, Lebanon
Services: Scheduled services from Beirut to destinations throughout the Middle East, North and West Africa, Europe, the Far East, Australia and South America. Points served include Abu Dhabi, Accra, Aden, Amman, Amsterdam, Athens, Baghdad, Bahrain, Berlin, Brussels, Bucharest, Cairo, Colombo, Copenhagen, Damascus, Dhahran, Doha, Dubai, Frankfurt, Freetown, Geneva, Istanbul, Kano, Khartoum, Kuala Lumpur, Kuwait, Lagos, Larnaca, London Heathrow, Madrid, Milan, Muscat, Nice, Paris CDG, Riyadh, Rome, São Paulo, Singapore, Sydney, Tunis and Zürich.
Fleet (14): 2 x Airbus A310-200, 2 x A310-300, 7 x Boeing 707-320C, 3 x 747-200C. *On order:* 2 x Airbus A320-200, 2 x A321-100.
Colour scheme: The renewal of the fleet is being accompanied by a modernised livery, introduced in late 1996. Its all white aircraft now carry 'MEA' initials in red, green and turquoise on the lower forward fuselage, and the airline name is repeated in full under the windowline at the rear, in the same colours, and in Arabic above, but in green throughout. The tailfin is dominated by a green cedar of Lebanon, mentioned in the Bible, which symbolises strength, holiness and eternity, while the red and white, taken from the national flag, stands for self-sacrifice and peace. The cedar is repeated on the engine cowlings.
Illustrated: MEA's fleet renewal is gaining momentum with the delivery of new Airbus twins, including this A320.

MONARCH AIRLINES (OM/MON)

Founded/First Service: 1 June 1967/5 April 1968

Base: Luton Airport, Luton, Bedfordshire, United Kingdom

Services: Extensive charter flights and inclusive tour packages for leading tour operators, including sister company Cosmos, from Luton, London Gatwick, Stansted, Manchester, Birmingham, Leeds Bradford and Glasgow to Europe and the Mediterranean area, as well as long-haul flights to such destinations as the United States, Bahamas, Mexico, Brazil, Kenya, Malaysia and Thailand. Also scheduled 'leisure' routes since July 1986 from Luton to Alicante, Mahon (Menorca), Malaga, Palma de Mallorca, and to Tenerife in the Canary Islands.

Fleet (25): 4 x Airbus A300-600R, 7 x A320-200, 8 x Boeing 757-200ER, 5 x 767-300ER (operated for Alitalia), 1 x McDonnell Douglas DC-10-30.

Colour scheme: A simple colour scheme with golden yellow and black 'straight through' cheatlines contrasts with the predominantly white fuselage and tail, which carries the company's crowned 'M' insignia. Bold black 'Monarch' titles appear behind the forward passenger door.

Illustrated: Monarch uses a single McDonnell Douglas DC-10-30, fitted out for 361 passengers, mainly between the UK and Orlando, Florida. *Terry Shone*

NIGERIA AIRWAYS (WT/NGA)

Founded/First Service: 1958/1 October 1958 as WAAC (Nigeria). Present title officially adopted 22 January 1972, but already used since foundation.

Base: Murtala Muhammed International Airport, Lagos, Nigeria

Services: Scheduled passenger and cargo services to destinations in East and West Africa and long-haul flights to Jeddah and London. Services to Amsterdam, Rome and New York are currently suspended. All points are served from Lagos, with some flights also from other bases at Kano and Port Harcourt. Extensive domestic route network takes in key cities in all 19 states.

Fleet (10): 2 x Airbus A310-200, 1 x Boeing 707-320C, 6 x 737-200A, 1 x McDonnell Douglas DC-10-30.

Colour scheme: The green and white colours of Nigeria Airways' corporate identity are taken from the national flag, signifying its role as the country's international flag carrier. The flag itself, where the green stands for agriculture and white for peace and unity, appears on the tailfin, superimposed by the airline's flying elephant symbol. Twin green cheatlines are separated by a narrow white windowline, underlining bold green 'NIGERIA AIRWAYS' titles in capital lettering. The white roof of the aircraft contrasts with the lower grey or natural metal fuselage.

Illustrated: The Boeing 737-200 Advanced flies most domestic services in Nigeria, with some excursions to neighbouring countries.

NORTHWEST AIRLINES (NW/NWA)

Founded/First Service: 1 August 1926/1 October 1926
Base: Minneapolis/St Paul International Airport, St Paul, Minnesota, USA
Services: Extensive passenger network within the United States, supplemented by feeder airlines operating under the 'Northwest Airlink' banner, and to Canada, Mexico and the Caribbean. Also trans-Pacific flights to the Far East, and across the Atlantic to London Gatwick, Glasgow, Amsterdam, Paris and Frankfurt. More than 390 cities served in 80 countries. Major hubs at Detroit, Minneapolis/St Paul, Memphis and Tokyo.
Fleet (397): 50 x Airbus A320-200, 47 x Boeing 727-200, 3 x 747-100, 20 x 747-200B, 8 x 747-200F, 10 x 747-400, 44 x 757-200, 22 x McDonnell Douglas DC-9-14/15, 106 x DC-9-31/32, 12 x DC-9-41, 35 x DC-9-51, 11 x DC-10-30, 21 x DC-10-40, 8 x MD-82.
On order: 20 x Airbus A320-200, 16 x A330-300, 4 x Boeing 747-400, 29 x 757-200.
Colour scheme: The Northwest corporate signature was introduced in June 1989. It focuses on an updated rendering of Northwest's call letters in white near the top of the tail expressing the 'N' explicitly, while the 'pointer' to its left strongly suggests the letter 'W' and a compass pointing northwest. The importance of the red tail is emphasised by extending the colour over the entire top of the fuselage above a strong presence of grey to communicate a note of seriousness and efficiency. A deep blue tapered speedstripe underscores the grey. Large 'NORTHWEST' lettering is applied in white on grey.

Illustrated: Long-haul services are shared between the growing DC-10 fleet and the Boeing 747s.

OLYMPIC AIRWAYS (OA/OAL)

Founded/First Service: 1 January 1957
Base: Athens Hellinikon International Airport, Athens, Greece
Services: Scheduled passenger and cargo services from Athens and a secondary hub at Thessaloniki to most major European and neighbouring Middle Eastern cities, as well as to destinations in Africa, the Far East, Australia and North America. Long-haul points are Bangkok, Boston, Johannesburg, Melbourne, Montreal, Nairobi, New York, Rio de Janeiro, São Paulo, Sydney and Toronto. Also extensive domestic route network serving 34 destinations, many flown by subsidiary, Olympic Aviation.
Fleet (35): 6 x Airbus A300B4-100, 2 x Airbus A300-600R, 5 x 727-200, 11 x 737-200, 7 x 737-400, 4 x 747-200B.
Olympic Aviation: 4 x ATR42-300, 7 x ATR72-200, 7 x Dornier Do228-200, 5 x Shorts 330-100 + light aircraft and helicopters.
Colour scheme: The famous six Olympic rings are painted in their traditional colours on the dark blue tailfin, which is an extension of the narrow cheatline carried above the windows. A broad sky blue windowline is underscored by orange and red 'straight through' pencil lines. Expanded 'OLYMPIC' lettering, also in dark blue, is carried on the forward half of the upper white fuselage behind a national blue and white pendant and the European Union flag.
Illustrated: Olympic took delivery of the first of two Airbus A300-600Rs in June 1992. They are configured for 269 passengers in a two-class layout.

PAKISTAN INTERNATIONAL AIRLINES — PIA (PK/PIA)

Founded/First Service: 1954/7 June 1954
Base: Quaid-i-Azam International Airport, Karachi, Pakistan
Services: More than 40 international destinations in Africa, Europe, Middle East and Far East, and the United States and Canada, together with a 35-point domestic network. European destinations are Amsterdam, Athens, Copenhagen, Frankfurt, Istanbul, London, Manchester, Moscow, Paris, Rome and Zürich. New York and Toronto are served in North America.
Fleet (46): 9 x Airbus A300B4-200, 6 x A310-300, 2 x Boeing 707-320C, 6 x 737-300, 8 x 747-200B(SCD), 2 x DHC-6 Twin Otter 300, 12 x Fokker F27-200, 1 x F27-400.
Colour scheme: The livery makes good use of the national colours of green and white, enhanced by two-tone green and light blue bands wrapped around the lower fuselage, starting just ahead of the wing. The green is continued over the whole underside to the rear of the fuselage, making for a most attractive and unusual scheme. 'Pakistan' titles in green, alongside their Urdu equivalent, are displayed on the upper forward fuselage. White 'PIA' initials highlight the all green tailfin.
Illustrated: PIA put the first of its six Airbus A310-300s into service in June 1991. They are used on services within Asia and to Europe.

93

PHILIPPINE AIRLINES — PAL (PR/PAL)

Founded/First Service: 25 February 1941/15 March 1941
Base: Ninoy Aquino International Airport, Manila, Philippines
Services: International passenger and cargo services to 34 cities in 23 countries, focusing on a strong regional route system, with long-haul flights across the Pacific to Honolulu, New York, San Francisco and Los Angeles, and westwards to Abu Dhabi, Cairo, Dubai, Dhahran, Frankfurt, Jeddah, Kuwait, London, Paris, Riyadh and Rome. Also vast domestic network linking Manila with 42 other points in the Philippine Islands.
Fleet (53): 12 x Airbus A300B4-100/200, 4 x A340-200, 12 x Boeing 737-300, 11 x 747-200B/C, 4 x 747-400, 10 x Fokker 50. *On order:* 12 x Airbus A320-200, 8 x A330-300, 8 x A340-300.
Colour scheme: The present livery was unveiled towards the end of 1986 and combines a stylish all-white fuselage finish with succinct solid blue 'Philippines' titling on the forward fuselage. The blue, white and red 'interlocking triangle' tail design inspired by the Philippine flag, features a sun bursting spectacularly from the red. The eight rays of the sun, also adopted from the flag, signify the first eight provinces to revolt against Spain during the independence movement in 1898.
Illustrated: An example of a Philippine Airlines A300B4.

QANTAS AIRWAYS (QF/QFA)

Founded/First Service: 16 November 1920
Base: Sydney Kingsford Smith Airport, Mascot, New South Wales, Australia
Services: Worldwide scheduled passenger and cargo services from Sydney and other state capitals serving 41 cities in 27 countries. Services to Europe take in Frankfurt, London, Manchester, Paris and Rome, while points in North America include Boston, Chicago, Los Angeles, New York, San Francisco, Toronto, Vancouver and Washington. Taipei is served by subsidiary, Australia Asia Airlines. Together with associate carriers also serves 52 towns and cities throughout Australia from seven gateways.
Fleet (97): 4 x Airbus A300B4-200, 16 x Boeing 737-300, 22 x 737-400,
5 x Boeing 747-200B(SCD), 6 x 747-300(EUD), 18 x 747-400, 2 x 747SP,
7 x 767-200ER, 17 x 767-300ER.
Colour scheme: The Qantas image is the work of Sydney design consultant Tony Lunn and Associates and was officially unveiled in June 1984. It features an all white fuselage with a strong tailfin arrangement, incorporating the white kangaroo symbol, in which the warm red is extended down around the fuselage. The red fin is trimmed in gold at the leading-edge for added elegance. The tail shape has been designed into triangular logos for the engine cowlings. Black 'QANTAS' titles are displayed near the forward passenger door, complemented by additional 'The Australian Airline' wording below, also in black.
Illustrated: The 747-400 Longreach, first delivered in August 1989, heads a fleet which comprises almost entirely Boeing aircraft.

REGIONAL AIRLINES (VM/RGI)

Founded/First Service: 1 January 1992 through merger of Air Vendee and Airlec
Base: Nantes-Atlantique Airport, Nantes, France
Services: Scheduled regional passenger and cargo services within France, radiating from Nantes, Bordeaux, Clermont-Ferrand, Lyon, Toulouse and Rouen, and extending across the borders to Amsterdam, Barcelona, Brussels, Frankfurt, Geneva, London, Manchester, Madrid, Milan and Porto. Domestic points are Angoulême, Bordeaux, Clermont-Ferrand, Caen, Dijon, Le Havre, Limoges, Lyon, Marseille, Nantes, Nice, Pau, Rouen, St Brieuc and Toulouse.
Fleet (22): 1 x ATR42-300, 8 x BAe Jetstream Super 31, 8 x Saab 340B, 5 x Saab 2000.
On order: 3 x Embraer EMB-145, 2 x Saab 2000.
Colour scheme: French navy and sky blue bands of different widths follow the line of the tail's leading-edge down and around the rear fuselage. Narrow stripes of the same colours are also applied to the engine cowlings. The company's logo, symbolising a gull flying over a graduated sky blue globe, appears in red near the top of the tail, and below the cockpit windows together with 'REGIONAL Airlines' titles. A large red gull with shortened 'Regional' titles is also displayed across the largely all white fuselage.
Illustrated: Regional Airlines' largest aircraft is the 50-seat Saab 2000 turboprop.

ROYAL AIR MAROC (AT/RAM)

Founded/First Service: 25 June 1953

Base: Mohammed V International Airport, Casablanca, Morocco

Services: Scheduled passenger and cargo services to North and West Africa, Middle East and Europe, as well as across the Atlantic to New York, Montreal and Rio de Janeiro. European cities served include Amsterdam, Athens, Barcelona, Bastia, Bordeaux, Brussels, Copenhagen, Düsseldorf, Frankfurt, Geneva, Istanbul, Lille, Lisbon, London, Lyon, Madrid, Malaga, Marseille, Milan, Munich, Nantes, Nice, Paris, Rome, Strasbourg, Toulouse, Vienna and Zürich. Also domestic flights including a frequent shuttle between Casablanca and Rabat.

Fleet (28): 2 x ATR42-300, 4 x Boeing 727-200A, 6 x 737-200A, 7 x 737-400, 5 x 737-500, 1 x 747-400, 1 x 747-200B(SCD), 2 x 757-200.

On order: 9 x Boeing 737-400.

Colour scheme: A green, white and red windowline separates the upper white fuselage from the grey underside. It tapers at both ends and promotes strong 'royal air maroc' titles in lower case red. The centrepiece of the red national flag is the green pentangle (or seal of Solomon), which adorns the tail in the form of a shooting star, whose red trail emanates from bold red 'RAM' initials at the base.

Illustrated: The Boeing 737-400 is the principal aircraft type used on domestic services and to nearby countries.

ROYAL BRUNEI AIRLINES (BI/RBA)

Founded/First Service: 18 November 1974/May 1975
Base: Bandar Seri Begawan Airport, Negara Darussalam Brunei
Services: Regional and long-haul passenger services to Abu Dhabi, Balikpapan, Bangkok, Beijing, Bintulu, Brisbane, Calcutta, Darwin, Denpasar/Bali, Dubai, Frankfurt, Hong Kong, Jakarta, Jeddah, Kota Kinabalu, Kuala Lumpur, Kuching, Labuan, London Heathrow, Manila, Miri, Osaka (Kansai), Perth, Singapore, Taipei and Yangon.
Fleet (15): 2 x Boeing 757-200ER, 9 x 767-300ER, 2 x Fokker 50, 2 x Fokker 100.
Colour scheme: Adopted in early 1986 to coincide with the delivery of its first Boeing 757, the airline's livery is based on the colours of the national flag, where yellow represents the Sultan and black and white his two chief ministers. The design features a yellow lower fuselage, separated from the white roof by pinstripes in yellow and black, and sweeping upwards over the tailfin. The national arms depicting a vertical winged support standing on the Muslim crescent, forms the main feature of the fin. Black 'ROYAL BRUNEI' titles are worn on the cabin roof alongside the national flag.
Illustrated: The airline's largely Boeing fleet is headed by nine 767-300ERs which operate all long-haul routes.

ROYAL JORDANIAN (RJ/RJA)

Founded/First Service: 8 December 1963/15 December 1963
Base: Queen Alia International Airport, Amman, Jordan
Services: Passenger and cargo services throughout the Middle East, the Far East, North Africa, Europe and the United States. Destinations beyond the Middle East include Amsterdam, Ankara, Athens, Bangkok, Berlin, Brussels, Cairo, Calcutta, Casablanca, Colombo, Frankfurt, Geneva, Istanbul, Jakarta, Kuala Lumpur, Larnaca, London, Madrid, Montreal, New York, Paris, Rome, Singapore, Toronto, Tunis and Vienna. Also a domestic flight between Amman and Aqaba.
Fleet (19): 2 x Airbus A310-200, 4 x A310-300, 3 x A320-200, 3 x Boeing 707-320C, 2 x 727-200A, 5 x Lockheed L1011 TriStar 50.
Colour scheme: The present livery, created by Landor Associates of San Francisco and introduced in 1986, was designed to convey a spirit of Jordan's heritage using majestic gold and red cheatlines along a unique charcoal grey upper fuselage. The gold crown of the Hashemite Kingdom dominates the tailfin, which also features subtle tapered speed bands in dark grey and a red tip. 'ROYAL JORDANIAN' titles in gold are applied along the cabin roof in both English and Arabic. The Jordanian flag, which incorporates a seven-pointed white star on a red field signifying the first seven verses of the Koran, is painted on the rear fuselage.
Illustrated: Pending a fleet renewal, Royal Jordanian continues to use two Boeing 727-200 Advanced trijets.

ROYAL NEPAL AIRLINES (RA/RNA)

Founded/First Service: 1 July 1958
Base: Tribhuvan Airport, Kathmandu, Nepal
Services: International scheduled flights from Kathmandu to Bangkok, Bombay, Calcutta, Delhi, Dhaka, Karachi, Dubai, Frankfurt, Hong Kong, Lhasa, Osaka (Kansai), Paris, London Gatwick, Shanghai, Singapore and Yangon. Vital domestic services provided to points on the southern slopes of the Himalayas and to isolated inland valleys totalling 37 destinations.
Fleet (14): 1 x Airbus A310-300, 2 x Boeing 757-200, 2 x BAe(HS) 748-2A/B, 8 x DHC-6 Twin Otter, 1 x Pilatus PC-6B/B1-H2 Turbo Porter.
Colour scheme: A pure white fuselage conveys the snow-capped peaks of the Himalayas, crossed by twin diagonal fin bands in the national colours of red and blue, which continue onto the rear fuselage. Blue 'Royal Nepal Airlines' titles are displayed on the forward cabin roof and preceded by the unusual 'double triangle' flag. The company's traditional winged Buddha symbol is painted beneath the cockpit windows.
Illustrated: The Boeing 757-200 enabled Royal Nepal Airlines to introduce long-haul services to Europe. It placed its first order in February 1986 and took delivery in September the following year.

Royal Nepal
Airlines

RYANAIR (FR/RYR)

Founded/First Service: May 1985
Base: Dublin Airport, Dublin, Ireland
Services: Scheduled passenger flights from the Irish Republic to points in the United Kingdom, linking Dublin to Birmingham, Bournemouth, Cardiff, Glasgow, Leeds Bradford, Liverpool, London (Gatwick and Stansted), Luton and Manchester; and London Stansted to Cork and Knock. Stansted is also linked to Glasgow/Prestwick, operated by Ryanair UK. Charter services from Dublin to European cities and resort areas.
Fleet (11): 11 x Boeing 737-200.
Colour scheme: A 'flying' variation of the Irish harp, which has been a national symbol since at least the 15th century, is displayed in yellow on a mid-blue tailfin. The mid-blue belly of the aircraft is separated from the otherwise white fuselage by a broad yellow band that dips down below the cockpit. Blue 'RYANAIR' titles are carried above the windowline forward of the wing, preceded by the yellow harp.
Illustrated: Ryanair now operates an all Boeing 737-200 twin-engined jet fleet. *James Lee*

SABENA WORLD AIRLINES (SN/SAB)

Founded/First Service: 23 March 1923
Base: Brussels National Airport, Zaventem, Belgium
Services: Comprehensive European scheduled services network and still expanding strong African presence, together with long-haul flights to Atlanta, Boston, Chicago and New York in the United States, and to Macau (in association with TAP Air Portugal) and to Tokyo in Japan, serving 90 cities. Some regional flights within Europe are flown by associate company, DAT Belgian Regional Airline (Delta Air Transport).
Fleet (39): 2 x Airbus A310-200, 1 x A310-300, 4 x A340-200,
13 x Boeing 737-200A, 6 x 737-300, 3 x 737-400, 6 x 737-500, 2 x 747-300 (SCD),
2 x McDonnell Douglas DC-10-30.
Colour scheme: The latest revamp to Sabena's classic livery was announced in April 1993. Developed in collaboration with Addison Design Consultancy of London to give the airline a warmer, more dynamic image, while remaining faithful to its traditions, the design highlights large faint silver 'sabena' lettering along the mid-fuselage, with traditional, but warmer blue titling forward. The letter 'S' on the tailplane has been redrawn and has been set into a circle with curved dynamic lines. The engine cowlings display the Belgian and European Union flags.
Illustrated: The Boeing 737 twinjet fleet, including this
737-200 Advanced, is used on intra-European services.

SAS SCANDINAVIAN AIRLINES SYSTEM (SK/SAS)

Founded/First Service: 31 July 1946
Bases: Arlanda Airport, Stockholm, Sweden; Fornebu Airport, Oslo, Norway and Copenhagen Airport, Denmark
Services: Extensive domestic and inter-Scandinavian network, together with services between Scandinavia and Europe, the Middle East and Far East, and the United States, serving more than 100 destinations in 32 countries. Scandinavian Commuter operates secondary routes with Fokker 50 turboprops using Norlink and Eurolink titles.
Fleet (155): 14 x 767-300ER, 16 x Fokker F28-4000, 3 x F28-1000, 22 x Fokker 50, 4 x McDonnell Douglas DC-9-21, 25 x DC-9-41, 32 x MD-81, 12 x MD-82, 4 x MD-83, 17 x MD-87, 6 x MD-90-30.
On order: 41 x Boeing 737-600, 2 x MD-90-30.
Scandinavian Commuter: 22 x Fokker 50. *On order:* 4 x Saab 2000.
Colour scheme: A rhombus in the national colours of the participating nations of Denmark, Norway and Sweden, in that order, provides a striking contrast to the fresh white overall fuselage as it wraps around the underside from window to window. Simple 'SCANDINAVIAN' titling in dark blue is shadowed in gold, as are the 'SAS' initials on the tail. The three national flags appear on the rear engines or the fuselage. The SAS livery was designed by Landor Associates and introduced from 1983.
Illustrated: The extended range Boeing 767-300ER flies all intercontinental routes.

SAUDI ARABIAN AIRLINES (SV/SVA)

Founded/First Service: 1945/4 March 1947
Base: King Abdul Aziz International Airport, Jeddah, Saudi Arabia
Services: Scheduled passenger services to more than 50 destinations in the Middle and Far East, Africa, Europe and the United States. Destinations in Europe are Amsterdam, Athens, Ankara, Frankfurt, Geneva, Istanbul, London, Madrid, Paris and Rome. Cargo flights to Brussels, Milan, Taipei and Tokyo. Also a 25-point domestic network.
Fleet (99): 11 x Airbus A300-600, 2 x Beechcraft A100 King Air,
2 x Boeing 707-320C, 20 x Boeing 737-200A, 8 x 747-100, 1 x 747-200B,
2 x 747-200F, 11 x 747-300, 3 x 747SP, 2 x Cessna 550 Citation II,
2 x Dassault Falcon 900, 1 x de Havilland Canada DHC-6 Twin Otter 300,
4 x Gulfstream II, 3 x Gulfstream III, 6 x Gulfstream IV, 17 x Lockheed L1011 TriStar 200, 2 x TriStar 500, 1 x McDonnell Douglas DC-8F-54, 1 x DC-8-63CF.
On order: 5 x 747-400, 23 x 777-200, 4 x MD-11F, 29 x MD-90-30.
Colour scheme: A new corporate identity was unveiled on 16 July 1996. The fuselage features selected shades of dune beige and white, separated by a gold pencil line, while the royal blue tail is dominated by a striking representation of the date palm and crossed swords in gold and enclosed by a golden crescent above a turquoise sea. 'SAUDI ARABIAN' titles are inscribed in English, followed by 'Al Saudia' (literally meaning, the airline is Saudi Arabia), in Arabic characters. The royal blue and turquoise colouring was inspired by the coral reefs and deep waters of the Red Sea and, together with the new rendering of the airline's symbol, were chosen to convey stature and dignity.
Illustrated: Saudia took delivery of its first Airbus A300-600 in March 1984. They are operated in a two-class configuration seating 258 passengers.

SINGAPORE AIRLINES (SQ/SIA)

Founded/First Service: 28 January 1972/1 October 1972
Base: Changi International Airport, Singapore
Services: Daily flights to 41 countries serving 74 cities in Europe, the Middle East, Asia, South West Pacific, Australia, New Zealand and North America. European destinations include Amsterdam, Athens, Berlin, Brussels, Copenhagen, Frankfurt, London, Madrid, Manchester, Paris, Rome, Vienna and Zürich. Freighter only services to Bangalore, Basle and Moscow. Subsidiary SilkAir serves 20 destinations in eight Asian countries.
Fleet (75): 6 x Airbus A310-200, 17 x A310-300, 4 x A340-300, 1 x 747-200F, 5 x 747-300, 3 x 747-300 (SCD), 34 x 747-400, 4 x 747-400F, 1 x Douglas DC-8F.
On order: 13 x Airbus A340-300, 12 x Boeing 747-400, 2 x 747-400F, 28 x 777-200.
Colour scheme: The all white fuselage displays dramatic foreshortened cheatlines in midnight blue and yellow, below blue 'SINGAPORE AIRLINES' titles. The lower yellow 'laser' line widens to the rear and is repeated on the vertical stabiliser in order to communicate precision. A large stylised yellow bird hovers on the otherwise blue tailfin and is repeated in miniature on each engine. The corporate identity was created by Landor Associates in 1972 and given a new logotype and other modifications in 1987.
Illustrated: SIA currently flies 38 Boeing 747-400 'Megatops'. If all orders and options are taken up, the fleet will eventually number 62 aircraft, including seven pure freighters.

SOUTH AFRICAN AIRWAYS — SAA (SA/SAA)

Founded/First Service: 1 February 1934

Base: Johannesburg International Airport, Johannesburg, Republic of South Africa.

Services: Intercontinental long-haul flights from Johannesburg, Cape Town and Durban to Amsterdam, Bangkok, Frankfurt, Hong Kong, Ilha do Sal, Lisbon, London, Miami, New York, Paris, Perth, Rio de Janeiro, Sydney, Taipei, Tel Aviv and Zürich. Regional services to Bulawayo, Harare, Lilongwe, Lusaka, Maputo, Mauritius, Nairobi, Victoria Falls and Windhoek. Also domestic trunk services.

Fleet (43): 4 x Airbus A300B2-3C, 2 x A300B4-200, 1 x A300C4-200, 7 x A320-200, 11 x Boeing 737-200A, 5 x 747-200B(SCD), 4 x 747-300, 4 x 747-400, 4 x 747SP, 1 x 767-200.

On order: 2 x Boeing 747-400, 4 x 777-200.

Colour scheme: SAA is finally sweeping away the last visible expression of the old political order and has revealed a new livery based on the national flag. Gone are the leaping springbok and House of Orange colours, which are being replaced on the tailfin by the new South African flag in black, gold and green, set between a blue field at the base and red at the top of the tail. The red encloses a golden sun disk, symbolising a new beginning. The fuselage is all-white with simple 'SOUTH AFRICAN' titles applied in blue on the forward fuselage.

Illustrated: A computer-generated image of South African Airways' new livery.

SWISSAIR (SR/SWR)

Founded/First Service: 16 March 1931
Base: Zürich Kloten Airport, Zürich, Switzerland
Services: Worldwide scheduled passenger and cargo network serving 125 destinations in 67 countries on all continents except Australia. Extensive European services reach all capitals together with many other major cities from Helsinki in the north to Malta in the south, while connections between Switzerland and the Americas reach Atlanta, Boston, Buenos Aires, Chicago, Cincinnati, Montreal, New York, Philadelphia, Rio de Janeiro, Santiago de Chile, São Paulo, Toronto and Washington, some served jointly with other carriers.
Fleet (78): 8 x A310-300, 5 x A319-100, 15 x A320-200, 8 x A321-100, 5 x Boeing 747-300(SCD), 10 x Fokker 100, 14 x McDonnell Douglas MD-11, 13 x MD-81.
On order: 3 x Airbus A319-100, 3 x A320-200, 2 x McDonnell Douglas MD-11.
Colour scheme: Like all Swiss airlines, Swissair is instantly recognisable by the white holy cross of the national flag which goes right back to the Battle of Laupen in 1339, and is emblazoned on a bright red tail. Bold red 'swissair' titles are carried on the forward white upper fuselage which extends down to wing level, giving way to a new purple underside. The twin cheatlines of brown and black have been replaced to give its aircraft a clean, modern look.
Illustrated: Swissair was an early customer for the Airbus A321, the largest version of the Airbus narrow-body family.

SYRIANAIR — SYRIAN ARAB AIRLINES (RB/SYR)

Founded/First Service: October 1961

Base: Damascus International Airport, Damascus, Syrian Arab Republic

Services: International scheduled passenger and cargo services to destinations within Syria and to points in Europe, North Africa, and the Middle and Far East. Cities on the network include Abu Dhabi, Algiers, Athens, Bahrain, Berlin Schönefeld, Bombay (Mumbai), Budapest, Cairo, Dhahran, Delhi, Doha, Dubai, Istanbul, Jeddah, Karachi, Kuwait, Larnaca, London, Madrid, Moscow, Munich, Paris, Prague, Riyadh, Rome, Sana'a, Sharjah, Sofia, Stockholm and Tunis.

Fleet (37): 1 x Antonov An-24V, 5 x An-26, 2 x Aerospatiale (Sud) Caravelle 10B3, 6 x Boeing 727-200, 2 x 747SP, 2 x Dassault Falcon 20F, 4 x Ilyushin Il-76M, 6 x Tupolev Tu-134B-3, 3 x Tu-154M, 6 x Yakovlev Yak-40.

Colour scheme: A bright Mediterranean blue windowline, trimmed with blue pinstripes above and below, extends the full length of the aircraft starting at the nose. It is surmounted by blue 'SYRIANAIR' titles in both English and Arabic. The company's symbol, a stylised mythical bird, flies across the sun on an otherwise blue tail.

Illustrated: Syrianair is considering modernising its fleet, but in the meantime continues to operate the Boeing 747SP on long-haul services.

TAP AIR PORTUGAL (TP/TAP)

Founded/First Service: 14 March 1945/September 1946
Base: Lisbon Airport, Lisbon, Portugal
Services: Extensive European network and flights to Africa, North and South America, and to Macau and China in association with partner airlines. European destinations are Amsterdam, Athens, Barcelona, Berlin, Bologna, Brussels, Cologne/Bonn, Copenhagen, Frankfurt, Geneva, Hamburg, Hannover, London, Luxembourg, Lyon, Madrid, Milan, Munich, Nice, Oslo, Paris, Rome, Stockholm, Stuttgart, Turin, Vienna and Zürich. A domestic route system includes Faro, Horta, Lisbon, Oporto, Ponta Delgada, Porto Santo and Terceira.
Fleet (35): 5 x Airbus A310-300, 6 x A320-200, 4 x A340-300, 6 x Boeing 737-200A, 10 x 737-300, 4 x Lockheed L1011 TriStar 500.
On order: 18 x Airbus A319.
Colour scheme: The red and white 'TAP' logo (from Transportes Aéreos Portugueses) flies up the white tail, followed by a red 'contrail' trimmed above in green, which forms the cheatline to the nose of the aircraft. The 't' in the 'tap' lettering appears in outline, while the others are in solid red. Black 'AIR PORTUGAL' titles on the cabin roof are preceded by the Portuguese flag. Green and red are the national colours of Portugal.
Illustrated: Air Portugal uses the Boeing 737-200 Advanced mainly on domestic services, including to Funchal on Madeira.

TAROM ROMANIAN AIRTRANSPORT (RO/ROT)

Founded/First Service: 1946 as TARS, present title adopted in 1954
Base: Otopeni International Airport, Bucharest, Romania
Services: Scheduled passenger services within Romania, and to points in Europe, Africa, the Middle East and Far East, and the United States. Cities served include Abu Dhabi, Amman, Amsterdam, Athens, Bahrain, Bangkok, Barcelona, Beijing, Berlin, Beirut, Bologna, Brussels, Budapest, Cairo, Calcutta, Chicago, Copenhagen, Damascus, Delhi, Dubai, Düsseldorf, Frankfurt, Istanbul, Karachi, Kiev, Kishinev, Kuwait, Larnaca, Lisbon, London, Madrid, Malé, Manchester, Moscow, New York, Paris, Prague, Rome, Sofia, Stockholm, Stuttgart, Tel Aviv, Thessalonika, Verona, Vienna, Warsaw and Zürich.
Fleet (37): 2 x Airbus A310-200, 14 x Antonov An-24RV, 5 x 737-300, 6 x British Aerospace (BAC) 1-11/500, 2 x Ilyushin Il-18D (F), 2 x IL-18V, 6 x Rombac 1-11/500.
On order: 1 x Airbus A310-200.
Colour scheme: The fleet comprises of a mixture of colour schemes, but the predominant design adopted displays large 'TAROM' titles in dark blue below the windowline and forward of the all white fuselage. The blue tail incorporates the airline's long-standing bird symbol, either in blue in a white double circle, or reversed out in white on a blue circle.
Illustrated: The Romanian flag carrier began its fleet modernisation programme in December 1992 with the delivery of two new Airbus A310s. *Terry Shone*

THAI AIRWAYS INTERNATIONAL (TG/THA)

Founded/First Service: 24 August 1959
Base: Don Muang International Airport, Bangkok, Thailand
Services: Extensive regional network and flights to Europe, North America and Australia and New Zealand, serving 51 cities in 36 countries. Long-haul destinations include Amsterdam, Athens, Auckland, Brisbane, Brussels, Copenhagen, Dubai, Frankfurt, Istanbul, London Heathrow, Los Angeles, Madrid, Melbourne, Muscat, Paris, Perth, Rome, Stockholm, Sydney and Zürich. Also comprehensive 20-point domestic system.
Fleet (75): 6 x Airbus A300-600, 10 x A300-600R, 7 x A300B4-200, 2 x A310-200, 8 x A330-300, 2 x ATR42-300, 2 x ATR72-200, 7 x Boeing 737-400, 6 x 747-200B, 2 x 747-300, 12 x 747-400, 4 x 777-200, 3 x McDonnell Douglas DC-10-30ER, 4 x MD-11.
On order: 4 x 777-200A.
Colour scheme: Thai's visual appearance was created by leading design consultants Landor Associates and introduced in 1975. Its rich and vibrant colours vividly reflect culture and country. Opulent gold, pink and purple tones recall the gold of the temples, the brilliant hues of the orchids and the intensity of Thailand's famous shimmering silks, all incorporated in an enormous stylised orchid symbol on the tail dominating the all-white fuselage. A smaller version speeds ahead of a gold, purple, gold cheatline, which runs the whole length of the aircraft. The abbreviated purple 'Thai' logo is displayed near the front passenger door.

Illustrated: Thai International's latest acquisition is the Rolls-Royce Trent-powered Boeing 777-200 twinjet.

TNT INTERNATIONAL AVIATION SERVICES (NTR)

Founded/First Service: 1946 (in Australia)/5 May 1987 (in Europe)

Services: Scheduled cargo services for its parent, TNT Express Worldwide, as well as contract and ad hoc charters concentrating on the thoroughbred racehorse industry. Current operators include Air Foyle, Pan Air of Spain, and Germany's Eurowings. Extensive European schedule flown five nights a week to many destinations, including Athens, Barcelona, Basle, Belfast, Billund, Birmingham, Bergamo, Brussels, Budapest, Cork, Dublin, Edinburgh, Geneva, Gothenburg, Helsinki, Istanbul, Leipzig, Liverpool, Lisbon, London Stansted, Lyon, Madrid, Malmö, Nuremberg, Oporto, Oslo, Paris CDG, Prague, Rome, Shannon, Stavanger, Stockholm, Valencia, Vienna, Warsaw, Waterford and Zaragoza. Pacific East Asia Cargo (PEAC) serves Hong Kong, Jakarta, Seoul, Singapore, Subic Bay and Taipei from Manila.

Fleet (24): 9 x British Aerospace 146-200QT, 9 x 146-300QT, 6 x Boeing 727-200 F.

Colour scheme: The standard scheme is a red 'TNT' embodied in three rectangles shown on the tailfin and forward fuselage, which is white over orange. Individual operators often include their logos/names on the engine cowlings or beneath the windscreens.

Illustrated: The BAe146-200QT and -300QT (Quiet Trader) all jet-powered freighters form the front-line fleet of TNT in Europe.

TRANSAERO AIRLINES (4J/TSO)

Founded/First Service: 28 December 1990
Base: Moscow Sheremetyevo Airport, Moscow, Russian Federation
Services: Scheduled passenger services within Russia, the CIS countries, Europe and the United States. Destinations include Almaty, Ashkhabad, Baku, Berlin Schönefeld, Cairo, Chicago, Eilat, Ekaterinburg, Frankfurt, Irkutsk, Kiev, Kishinev, London, Minsk, Nizhnevartovsk, Novosibirsk, Norlisk, Odessa, Orlando, Riga, Sochi, St Petersburg, Tashkent, Tel Aviv, Vladivostok and Yuzho-Sakhalinsk. Feeder services within Russia by subsidiary Transaero Express.
Fleet (12): 5 x Boeing 737-200A, 5 x 757-200, 1 x Ilyushin IL-86,
1 x McDonnell Douglas DC-10-30.
Colour scheme: The simple livery of Russia's second international airline comprises a red graduated arrow in the national colours of red and blue flying up the white tailfin, and blue 'TRANSAERO' titles on the forward cabin roof. The upper fuselage of the aircraft is arctic white, going over into a grey lower half just below the windowline.
Illustrated: The almost entirely Western fleet comprises the Boeing 757-200, used on longer sectors within Russia and to destinations in Europe.

TRANSAVIA AIRLINES (HV/TRA)

Founded/First Service: 1965/16 November 1966
Base: Schiphol Airport, Amsterdam, The Netherlands
Services: Scheduled passenger services from Amsterdam to London Gatwick, and to the resorts of Alicante, Faro, Funchal, Heraklion, Larnaca, Las Palmas de Gran Canaria, Malaga, Malta, Palma de Mallorca, Tenerife and Tunis. Also extensive holiday charter flights to some 60 destinations in Europe, flown mostly for French, German and Italian tour operators. Spare capacity leased out to other operators.
Fleet (18): 14 x Boeing 737-300, 4 x 757-200.
On order: 8 x Boeing 737-800.
Colour scheme: A new corporate identity was introduced on 20 February 1995. Developed in co-operation with more than 200 employees, the new scheme emphasises such concepts as strength, dynamism, enthusiasm and personal attention. A bold green flash sweeps from nose to tail on a brilliant white fuselage, ending in an elegant stylised 'T' in blue and green on the white tail. Blue 'Transavia' titles are placed above the forward cabin windows and repeated on the outboard face of the white engine cowlings. Since autumn 1996, a sticker close to the forward door emphasises the airline's membership of the KLM Group.
Illustrated: The Boeing 737-300 in the new livery catches the sun over a grey North Sea.

TRANS WORLD AIRLINES — TWA (TW/TWA)

Founded/First Service: 13 July 1925/17 April 1926
Bases: John F. Kennedy International Airport, New York and Lambert St Louis Airport, St Louis, Missouri, United States
Services: Extensive domestic trunk services, together with Caribbean flights to Cancun, Ixtapa/Zihuatanejo, Mexico City, Montego Bay, Puerto Vallarta, San Juan and Santo Domingo, and trans-Atlantic routings to Europe, North Africa and the Middle East, serving Athens, Barcelona, Cairo, Frankfurt, Lisbon, London, Madrid, Milan, Paris, Riyadh, Rome and Tel Aviv. Feeder services from more than 40 points in the US are provided under the Trans World Express banner by subsidiary Trans States Airlines.
Fleet (192): 41 x Boeing 727-200A, 9 x 747-100, 2 x 747-200B, 5 x 757-200, 12 x 767-200ER, 3 x 767-300ER, 9 x Lockheed L1011 TriStar 1, 2 x L1011 TriStar 50, 3 x L1011 TriStar 100, 7 x McDonnell Douglas DC-9-15, 35 x DC-9-30, 1 x DC-9-33F, 3 x DC-9-41, 12 x DC-9-51, 29 x MD-82, 19 x MD-83.
On order: 10 x Airbus A330-300, 15 x Boeing 757-200.
Colour scheme: TWA's latest livery was introduced with the delivery of the first Boeing 757 in July 1996. A broad warm red and thinner gold cheatline sit atop the midnight blue of the underside of the aircraft and provide separation from the snow-white top. The three colours extend up the rear of the tailfin, supporting the traditional 'TWA' lettering. Elegantly understated 'TRANS WORLD' titles end in a stylised golden globe.
Illustrated: The airline's re-equipment programme, begun in summer 1996, is headed by the twin-engined Boeing 757-200.

TUNIS AIR (TU/TAR)

Founded/First Service: 1948
Base: Carthage International Airport, Tunis, Tunisia
Services: International scheduled services linking Tunis to destinations in Europe, the Middle East and North and West Africa. Points served include Abu Dhabi, Algiers, Amman, Amsterdam, Athens, Barcelona, Berlin Schönefeld, Bordeaux, Brussels, Cairo, Casablanca, Copenhagen, Dakar, Damascus, Düsseldorf, Frankfurt, Geneva, Hamburg, Istanbul, Jeddah, Lille, Lisbon, London, Lyon, Madrid, Marseille, Milan, Munich, Nice, Nouakchott, Palermo, Paris Orly, Prague, Rome, Strasbourg, Toulouse, Vienna, Warsaw and Zürich. Inclusive-tour charters to principal tourist gateways of Djerba and Monastir.
Fleet (24): 1 x Airbus A300B4-200, 8 x A320-200, 7 x Boeing 727-200A, 4 x 737-200A, 4 x 737-500.
Colour scheme: The latest livery was adopted with the introduction into service of the Airbus A320 in October 1990. It is centred on an all-white fuselage highlighted by a red flying gazelle on the tailfin. The impression of speed has

TURKISH AIRLINES — THY (TK/THY)

Founded/First Service: 20 May 1933 as Devlet Hava Yollari
Base: Yesilkoy Airport, Istanbul, Turkey
Services: International routes serving 56 cities, with strong emphasis on European network, which links Istanbul and Ankara with 34 destinations. Points served in Central Asia, North Africa, Middle East, Far East and the United States are Abu Dhabi, Ashkhabad, Almaty, Amman, Bahrain, Baku, Bangkok, Beijing, Beirut, Bombay (Mumbai), Cairo, Damascus, Dubai, Delhi, Jeddah, Karachi, Kuala Lumpur, Kuwait, New York/JFK, Riyadh, Singapore, Tashkent, Tehran, Tunis and Tokyo. Dense domestic network encompasses 26 towns and cities.
Fleet (65): 7 x Airbus A310-200, 7 x A310-300, 4 x A340-300, 10 x Avro RJ100, 2 x RJ70, 3 x Boeing 727-200C, 30 x 737-400, 2 x 737-500.
On order: 1 x Airbus A340-300.
Colour scheme: The national colours of red and white predominate on the latest

TYROLEAN AIRWAYS (VO/TYR)

Founded/First Service: 1979/9 April 1980
Base: Innsbruck Kranebitten Airport, Innsbruck, Tyrol, Austria
Services: Extensive European regional network linking various Austrian cities with Amsterdam, Bologna, Budapest, Brussels, Cologne/Bonn, Dresden, Düsseldorf, Florence, Frankfurt, Hamburg, Hannover, Kosice, Krakow, Leipzig, Ljubljana, Madrid, Munich, Nuremberg, Paris, Prague, Stuttgart, Timisoara, Venice, Zagreb and Zürich. Domestic flights serving Graz, Innsbruck, Klagenfurt, Linz and Vienna.
Fleet (28): 7 x Canadair Regional Jet 200LR, 1 x de Havilland Canada DHC-7, 6 x DHC-8-100, 11 x DHC-8-300, 3 x Fokker 70.
On order: 4 x de Havilland Canada DHC-8-400.
Colour scheme: Focal point of the Tyrolean livery is the triple arrow-shaped company colour motif of deep red, orange and bright yellow, introduced in mid-1985 and modified subtly in the meantime. The three colours appear diagonally across half of the tailfin, underscored by 'tyrolean' titles in black, and are

been created with red pinstripes trailing down the fin and around the rear fuselage. Red 'TUNISAIR' titles in English and Arabic are displayed on the cabin roof, with the Tunisian flag near the rear.

Illustrated: The most modern aircraft in the airline's fleet is the twin-engined Airbus A320 which will gradually replace the older Boeing 727-200s.

scheme, with a red tailfin riding the all white fuselage. Set into a white circle on the fin is the airline's bird symbol in red. Blue 'TURKISH' titles are followed by a small Turkish flag which includes the crescent moon and star on a red field, associated with the Ottoman Empire. All aircraft carry names of Turkish towns and cities.

Illustrated: An A310-300 of the Turkish Airlines fleet.

repeated on the underside at the rear of the all white fuselage and on the wingtips. The airline title, preceded by the three-colour arrow symbol, is duplicated above the forward cabin windows.

Illustrated: Tyrolean Airways acquired the Fokker 70 alongside its partner Austrian Airlines in summer 1995. It is operated in a 2/3-abreast configuration for 80 passengers on its main European services.

UKRAINE INTERNATIONAL AIRLINES (PS/AUI)

Founded/First Service: October 1992/November 1992
Base: Borispol Airport, Kiev, Ukraine
Services: International scheduled passenger services between Kiev and Amsterdam, Berlin, Brussels, Frankfurt, London Gatwick, Madrid, Manchester, Munich, Paris, Vienna and Zürich. The Manchester service is flown via Lvov. Also new domestic route from Kiev to Donetsk.
Fleet (4): 1 x Antonov An-24V, 2 x Boeing 737-200, 1 x 737-300.
Colour scheme: Ukraine International Airlines uses the national colours of blue and yellow to good effect. The blue of the tailfin is carried down in line with the leading-edge and wrapped around the fuselage behind a broad band of yellow. A highly stylised bird symbol flies on a yellow disk set into the blue tail. 'Ukraine International' titles, preceded by the national flag, are carried on the forward fuselage above the windowline, while the full title appears in the local language below the windows.
Illustrated: Ukraine International Airlines, which was set up by the Ukrainian Government with the assistance of GPA, is leasing three Boeing 737s for overseas flag services. The 737-300 is configured in a two-class, Business/Economy 'flexible interior' layout for 132 passengers.

UNITED AIRLINES (UA/UAL)

Founded/First Service: 1 July 1931
Base: Chicago O'Hare International Airport, Chicago, Illinois, USA
Services: Scheduled passenger and cargo services to 39 international destinations and two US territories in Canada, Central America, Europe, the Far East and Australasia, plus 98 airports in the United States. Another 185 cities served in the US by its United Express partners. Destinations in Europe are Amsterdam, Brussels, Düsseldorf, Frankfurt, London Heathrow, Milan, Paris/CDG and Zürich, served variously from Chicago, Washington DC and several other US cities. Round the world service linking Los Angeles, New York, London, Delhi and Hong Kong.
Fleet (564): 34 x Airbus A320-200, 75 x Boeing 727-200A, 67 x 737-200, 101 x 737-300, 57 x 737-500, 17 x 747-100, 9 x 747-200B, 24 x 747-400, 90 x 757-200, 19 x 767-200, 23 x 767-300ER, 14 x 777-200, 26 x McDonnell Douglas DC-10-10, 8 x DC-10-30.
On order: 16 x A320-200, 2 x 747-400, 2 x 757-200, 20 x 777-200.
Colour scheme: United's elegant business-like scheme features a combination of a silver-grey upper fuselage and a striped tailfin with alternative mid-blue and dark blue stripes. The blue and red corporate 'double U' outlined in white, is set into the top half of the fin. Triple pinstripes in orange, red and blue separate the upper fuselage from the deep midnight blue belly of the aircraft. White 'UNITED AIRLINES' titles are displayed at the front.
Illustrated: Launch customer United now has 14 Boeing 777 twinjets in service, with another 20 on firm order, plus 34 on option.

UNITED PARCEL SERVICE — UPS (5X/UPS)

Founded/First Service: 1983
Base: Louisville, Kentucky, United States
Services: Worldwide cargo and package delivery services to more than 200 countries, offering next day and two-day delivery service to anywhere in the world. Major hubs and distribution points include Bergamo, Cologne/Bonn, East Midlands, Guadalajara, Hamilton, Hong Kong, Louisville, Mexico City, Montreal, Monterrey, Nuremberg, Porto, Rome, Seoul, Singapore, Taipei, Tokyo/Narita, Vienna and Zaragoza.
Fleet (186): 51 x Boeing 727-100, 8 x 727-200A, 15 x 747-100F, 55 x 757-200PF, 5 x 767-300ER, 24 x McDonnell Douglas DC-8-71F, 28 x DC-8-73F.
On order: 10 x Boeing 757-200PF, 30 x 767-300F.
Colour scheme: Using a dark chocolate brown as the predominant colour, the UPS scheme displays a traditional 'straight through' windowline which extends at the rear to fill the tailfin. The company shield, displaying 'UPS' lettering beneath a 'wrapped parcel', appears in gold outline on the tail. Bold brown 'United Parcel Service' lettering is carried on the forward upper fuselage.
Illustrated: The Boeing 727 and 757PF (Package Freighter) make up the largest element of the fleet, totalling more than 100 aircraft.

US AIRWAYS (US/USA)

Founded/First Service: 5 March 1937 as All-American Aviation/13 September 1937. From 1953 known as Allegheny Airlines, USAir title adopted 28 October 1979. Renamed 27 February 1997.

Bases: Pittsburgh International Airport, Pennsylvania and Douglas Municipal Airport, Charlotte, North Carolina, United States

Services: Vast domestic network connecting 210 destinations throughout the United States, plus Montreal, Ottawa and Toronto in Canada, and the Bahamas, Bermuda, Grand Cayman, Jamaica, Mexico, Netherlands Antilles and San Juan, Puerto Rico. Trans-Atlantic flights serve Frankfurt, Madrid, Munich, Paris and Rome. Ten local carriers provide feeder services to domestic hubs under the USAir Express banner. Piedmont, PSA and Trans States are USAir subsidiaries.

Fleet (392): 64 x Boeing 737-200A, 85 x 737-300, 54 x 737-400, 34 x 757-200, 12 x 767-200ER, 8 x Fokker F28-4000, 40 x Fokker 100, 64 x McDonnell Douglas DC-9-31/32, 19 x MD-81, 12 x MD-82.

Colour scheme: With the official change of name from USAir to US Airways on 27 February 1997, the airline is changing its livery to reflect its experience as an international airline. Designed by New York-based Deskey Design Associates, the aircraft feature a near midnight blue upper fuselage, separated from the lower grey by narrow red and white cheatlines below the windows. The blue extends up to cover most of the trailfin, which is topped again by white and red, and displays a stylised flag in grey. This also appears ahead of the US AIRWAYS titles along mid-fuselage. Associated regional carriers' aircraft will adopt a similar scheme, with the word 'Express' below US AIRWAYS , usually applied below the cockpit windows.

Illustrated: USAir uses its Boeing 767-200ER across the North Atlantic. Its fleet of nearly 400 aircraft is being repainted in the new colours, a process which will take some three years to complete.

UZBEKISTAN AIRWAYS (HY/UZB)

Founded/First Service: 28 January 1992

Bases: Yuzhnyy International Airport, Tashkent and Samarkand Airport, Uzbekistan

Services: International scheduled services from Tashkent and Samarkand to Europe, the Middle and Far East, and the United States, serving Amsterdam, Athens, Bahrain, Bangkok, Beijing, Frankfurt, Istanbul, Jeddah, Karachi, London, Male, Manchester, New Delhi, New York, Kuala Lumpur, Seoul, Sharjah and Tel Aviv. Extensive domestic flights and schedules to most of the Commonwealth of Independent States (CIS) also operated.

Fleet (412): 2 x Airbus A310-300, 223 x Antonov An-2, 20 x An-24V, 4 x An-24RV, 2 x Boeing 767-300ER, 4 x Ilyushin IL-62, 8 x IL-62M, 14 x IL-76TD, 10 x IL-86, 39 x Kamov Ka-32, 18 x Mil Mi-2, 17 x Mi-8, 21 x Tupolev Tu-154B/B-1/B-2, 2 x Tu-154M, 28 x Yakovlev Yak-40.

Colour scheme: A sky blue fuselage roof and grass green belly, both outlined by a red pencil line and starting behind the cockpit, frame the white mid-part of the fuselage, sporting black 'UZBEKISTAN' titles. The fuselage paint scheme closely mirrors the national flag. The sky blue tail features the airline logo of a stylised dove in green, within a gold disk encircled in red. The logo is also displayed on the blue engine cowlings.

Illustrated: The Airline's first Western Aircraft in the shape of two airbus A310-300s were delivered in 1993.

VARIG BRAZILIAN AIRLINES (RG/VRG)

Founded/First Service: 7 May 1927/3 February 1928
Base: Galeao International Airport, Rio de Janeiro, Brazil
Services: Extensive domestic and regional scheduled passenger and cargo services, as well as intercontinental long-haul flights to destinations in Europe, West Africa, southern Africa, the Far East, Mexico and the United States, serving 30 destinations in 23 countries. Trans-Atlantic and trans-Pacific points served are Amsterdam, Bangkok, Copenhagen, Frankfurt, Hong Kong, Johannesburg, Lisbon, London, Madrid, Milan, Nagoya, Paris, Porto, Rome, Tokyo and Zürich. US destinations are Atlanta, Los Angeles, and Miami.
Fleet (81): 5 x Boeing 727-100C, 17 x 737-200A, 25 x 737-300, 3 x 747-200B(SCD), 5 x 747-300(SCD), 6 x 767-200ER, 4 x 767-300ER, 6 x McDonnell Douglas MD-11, 10 x DC-10-30/CF.
On order: 10 x Boeing 737-300, 6 x 747-400.
Colour scheme: Brazil's flag carrier introduced a new corporate identity in late 1996. It is distinguished by a navy blue tailfin, underbelly accented with a lighter blue and engine cowlings, framing the crisp white aircraft fuselage. The airline's long-standing compass insignia has been restyled in two hues of yellow, suggesting the warmth of the sun and the lustre of the gold.
Traditional 'VARIG' titles in matching blue are followed by 'BRASIL' in gold script. A small representation of the Brazilian flag is painted on the rear fuselage near the aircraft registration. The new identity is said to represent success, dynamism and the 'Brazilian spirit'.
Illustrated: The Boeing 747 was the first aircraft to be painted in Varig's new colours.

VIRGIN ATLANTIC AIRWAYS (VS/VIR)

Founded/First Service: June 1982/22 June 1984
Bases: London Gatwick and Heathrow Airports, United Kingdom
Services: Scheduled value-for-money passenger services from London Heathrow to Hong Kong, Johannesburg, Los Angeles, New York (Newark and JFK International Airports), San Francisco and Tokyo. Services from London Gatwick link Boston, Miami, and Orlando, which is also served from Manchester, while Athens is served from both London airports. A European subsidiary based at Brussels operates under the Virgin Express title.
Fleet (16): 1 x Airbus A320-200, 6 x A340-300,
1 x Boeing 747-100, 5 x 747-200B, 3 x 747-400.
On order: 1 x Airbus A340-300.
Colour scheme: A simple 'straight through' windowline in orange-red divides the all white fuselage and leads to the orange-red tailfin. The well-known 'Virgin' signature appears in white on the fin and in a smaller red version under the cockpit windows. Distinctive features are the red engine cowlings and red winglets on the Airbuses and Boeing 747-400s.
Illustrated: Virgin was the first and to date only airline in the UK to introduce the new Airbus A340, taking delivery of the first aircraft in December 1993. They are configured for 253 passengers in a three-class layout.

Aircraft Nationality and Registration Marks

An organised systematic approach to the registration of civil aircraft was first proposed as early as 1912 but, due to the intervention of World War 1, it was not instituted until the Paris Air Convention in 1919. It was then recommended that all aircraft should have five letters, with the first denoting the nationality. All letters were to be painted in black on white as large as possible on both sides of the fuselage as well as on the top surface and underside of the wings. In addition, the nationality letter was to be painted on each side of the tailplane. Privately-owned aircraft had to have the last four letters underlined.

As a result of the rapid development of civil aviation, almost all countries owned aircraft by 1929 and the regulations were revised accordingly. Gradually however, many of these rules were forgotten, with registrations becoming smaller and the nationality letter on the tail disappearing altogether. The present standards, adopted by ICAO on 8 February 1949, call for registrations to be applied on the upper half of the vertical tail surface, but this is rarely being adhered to. They should also be clean, clearly visible and identifiable.

With the exception of the national prefix, which has been adopted by all the member nations, the individual aircraft registration is issued subject to the country's own internal regulations for civil aircraft. These are usually in the form of three or four letters (depending on whether a one or two-letter national prefix is allocated) either in alphabetical or numerical sequence. Some nations have their own subdivisions which serve to group individual aircraft types and thus assist in recognition (eg SE-H for helicopters). In many countries, major airlines are given a special sequence which makes them instantly recognisable; such examples are ZS-SA for South African Airways, HS-T for Thai International, etc.

List of aircraft nationality registrations notified to the International Civil Aviation Organisation (ICAO)

Afghanistan	YA	Botswana	A2
Albania	ZA	Brazil	PP, PR, PT, PU
Algeria	7T	British Virgin Islands	VP-LV
American Samoa	N	Brunei	V8
Andorra	C3	Bulgaria	LZ
Angola	D2	Burkina Faso	XT
Anguilla	VP-LA	Burundi	9U
Antigua	V2	Cambodia	XU
Argentina	LV, LQ	Cameroon	TJ
Armenia	EK	Canada	C, CF
Aruba	P4	Cape Verde Republic	D4
Australia	VH	Caroline Islands	N
Austria	OE	Cayman Islands	VR-C
Azerbaijan	4K	Central African Republic	TL
Bahamas	C6	Chad	TT
Bahrain	A9C	Chile	CC
Bangladesh	S2	China (People's Republic)	B
Barbados	8P	China/Taiwan (Republic of China)	B
Barbuda	V2	Colombia	HK
Belarus	EW	Comoro Republic	D6
Belau (Palau)	-	Congo	TN
Belgium	OO	Costa Rica	TI
Belize	V3	Croatia	9A
Benin	TY	Cuba	CU
Bermuda	VR-B	Cyprus	5B
Bhutan	A5	Czech Republic	OK
Bolivia	CP	Denmark	OY
Bosnia-Herzegovina	T9	Djibouti	J2

Dominica	J7
Dominican Republic	HI
Ecuador	HC
Egypt	SU
El Salvador	YS
Equatorial Guinea	3C
Eritrea	E3
Estonia	ES
Ethiopia	ET
Falkland Islands	VP-F
Fiji	DQ
Finland	OH
France	F
French Overseas Departments	F-O
Gabon	TR
Gambia	C5
Georgia	4L
Germany	D
Ghana	9G
Gibraltar	VR-G
Greece	SX
Grenada	J3
Grenadines	J8
Guadeloupe	F-O
Guam	N
Guatemala	TG
Guinea	3X
Guinea Bissau	J5
Guyana	8R
Guyane	F-O
Haiti	HH
Honduras	HR
Hong Kong	VR-H
Hungary	HA
Iceland	TF
India	VT
Indonesia	PK
Iran	EP
Iraq	YI
Ireland	EI, EJ
Israel	4X
Italy	I
Ivory Coast	TU
Jamaica	6Y
Japan	JA
Jordan	JY
Kazakhstan	UN
Kenya	5Y
Kiribati	T3
Korea (Democratic People's Republic) (North Korea)	P
Korea (Republic of) (South Korea)	HL
Kuwait	9K
Kyrgyzstan	EX
Laos	RDPL
Latvia	YL
Lebanon	OD
Lesotho	7P
Liberia	EL
Libyan Arab Jamahiriya	5A
Liechtenstein	HB
Lithuania	LY
Luxembourg	LX

Macedonia	Z3
Malagasy Republic (Madagascar)	5R
Malawi	7Q
Malaysia	9M
Mali	TZ
Maldives	8Q
Malta	9H
Mariana Islands	N
Marshall Islands	V7
Martinique	F-O
Mauritania	5T
Mauritius	3B
Mexico	XA, XB, XC
Moldova	ER
Monaco	3A
Mongolia	MT
Montserrat	VP-LM to VP-LUZ
Morocco	CN
Mozambique	C9
Myanmar	XY, XZ
Namibia	V5
Nauru	C2
Nepal	9N
Netherlands	PH
Netherlands Antilles	PJ
Nevis	V4
New Caledonia	F-O
New Zealand	ZK, ZL, ZM
Nicaragua	YN
Niger	5U
Nigeria	5N
Norway	LN
Oman	A40
Pakistan	AP
Palau (Belau)	-
Panama	HP
Papua New Guinea	P2
Paraguay	ZP
Peru	OB
Philippines	RP
Poland	SP
Polynesia	F-O
Portugal	CR, CS
Puerto Rico	N
Qatar	A7
Réunion	F-O
Romania	YR
Russian Federation	RA
Rwanda	9XR
Saint-Barthelemy	F-O
St Helena/Ascension Island	VQ-H
St Kitts and Nevis	V4
St Lucia	J6
Saint-Pierre & Miquelon	F-O
St Vincent & Grenadines	J8
San Marino	T7
Sao Tomé and Principe	S9
Saudi Arabia	HZ
Senegal	6V, 6W
Serbia	YU
Seychelles	S7
Sierra Leone	9L
Singapore	9V

Slovakia	OM	CX	Uruguay
Slovenia	S5	C2	Nauru
Solomon Islands	H4	C3	Andorra
Somalia	6O	C5	Gambia
South Africa	ZS, ZT, ZU	C6	Bahamas
Spain	EC	C9	Mozambique
Sri Lanka	4R	D	Germany
Sudan	ST	DQ	Fiji
Suriname	PZ	D2	Angola
Swaziland	3D	D4	Cape Verde Republic
Sweden	SE	D6	Comoro Republic
Switzerland	HB	EC	Spain
Syria	YK	EI	Ireland
Tajikistan	EY	EK	Armenia
Tanzania	5H	EL	Liberia
Thailand	HS	EP	Iran
Togo	5V	ER	Moldova
Tonga	A3	ES	Estonia
Trinidad & Tobago	9Y	ET	Ethiopia
Tunisia	TS	EW	Belarus
Turkey	TC	EX	Kyrgyzstan
Turkmenistan	EZ	EY	Tajikistan
Turks & Caicos Islands	VQ-T	EZ	Turkmenistan
Tuvalu	T2	E3	Eritrea
Uganda	5X	F	France
Ukraine	UR	F-O	French Overseas Departments
United Arab Emirates	A6	G	United Kingdom
United Kingdom	G	HA	Hungary
United Kingdom Dependencies	VP, VQ, VR	HB	Switzerland & Liechtenstein
United Nations Organisation	4U	HC	Ecuador
Uruguay	CX	HH	Haiti
United States of America	N	HI	Dominican Republic
US Virgin Islands	N	HK	Colombia
Uzbekistan	UK	HL	Republic of Korea
Vanuatu	YJ	HP	Panama
Vatican	HV	HR	Honduras
Venezuela	YV	HS	Thailand
Vietnam	VN	HV	The Vatican
Virgin Islands (British)	VP-LV	HZ	Saudi Arabia
Virgin Islands (US)	N	H4	Solomon Islands
Western Samoa	5W	I	Italy
Yemen	7O	JA	Japan
Zaire	9Q	JY	Jordan
Zambia	9J	J2	Djibouti
Zimbabwe	Z	J3	Grenada
		J5	Guinea Bissau
		J6	St Lucia
		J7	Dominica
AP	Pakistan	J8	St Vincent & Grenadines
A2	Botswana	LN	Norway
A3	Tonga	LQ, LV	Argentina
A40	Oman	LX	Luxembourg
A5	Bhutan	LY	Lithuania
A6	United Arab Emirates	LZ	Bulgaria
A7	Qatar	MT	Mongolia
A9C	Bahrain	N	United States of America
B	China (People's Republic)	OB	Peru
B	China/Taiwan (Republic of China)	OD	Lebanon
C, CF	Canada	OE	Austria
CC	Chile	OH	Finland
CN	Morocco	OK	Czech Republic
CP	Bolivia	OM	Slovakia
CS	Portugal	OO	Belgium
CU	Cuba		

OY	Denmark
P	Korea (Democratic People's Republic) (North Korea)
PH	Netherlands
PJ	Netherlands Antilles
PK	Indonesia
PP, PR, PT, PU	Brazil
PZ	Suriname
P2	Papua New Guinea
P4	Aruba
RA	Russia
RDPL	Laos
RP	Philippines
SE	Sweden
SP	Poland
ST	Sudan
SU	Egypt
SX	Greece
S2	Bangladesh
S5	Slovenia
S7	Seychelles
S9	Sao Tomé and Principe
TC	Turkey
TF	Iceland
TG	Guatemala
TI	Costa Rica
TJ	Cameroon
TL	Central African Republic
TN	Congo
TR	Gabon
TS	Tunisia
TT	Chad
TU	Ivory Coast
TY	Benin
TZ	Mali
T2	Tuvalu
T3	Kiribati
T7	San Marino
T9	Bosnia-Herzegovina
UK	Uzbekistan
UN	Kazakhstan
UR	Ukraine
VH	Australia
VN	Vietnam
VP-F	Falkland Islands
VP-LA	Anguilla
VP-LM	Montserrat
VP-LV	British Virgin Islands
VQ-H	St Helena/Ascension Island
VQ-T	Turks & Caicos Islands
VR-B	Bermuda
VR-C	Cayman Islands
VR-G	Gibraltar
VR-H	Hong Kong
VT	India
V2	Antigua & Barbuda
V3	Belize
V4	St Kitts & Nevis
V5	Namibia
V7	Marshall Islands
V8	Brunei
XA, XB, XC	Mexico
XT	Burkina Faso

XU	Cambodia
XY, XZ	Myanmar
YA	Afghanistan
YI	Iraq
YJ	Vanuatu
YK	Syria
YL	Latvia
YN	Nicaragua
YR	Romania
YS	El Salvador
YU	Serbia
YV	Venezuela
Z	Zimbabwe
ZA	Albania
ZK, ZL, ZM	New Zealand
ZP	Paraguay
ZS, ZT, ZU	South Africa
Z3	Macedonia
3A	Monaco
3B	Mauritius
3C	Equatorial Guinea
3D	Swaziland
3X	Guinea
4K	Azerbaijan
4L	Georgia
4R	Sri Lanka
4U	United Nations Organisation
4X	Israel
5A	Libya
5B	Cyprus
5H	Tanzania
5N	Nigeria
5R	Malagasy Republic (Madagascar)
5T	Mauritania
5U	Niger
5V	Togo
5W	Western Samoa
5X	Uganda
5Y	Kenya
6O	Somalia
6V, 6W	Senegal
6Y	Jamaica
7O	Yemen
7P	Lesotho
7Q	Malawi
7T	Algeria
8P	Barbados
8Q	Maldives
8R	Guyana
9A	Croatia
9G	Ghana
9H	Malta
9J	Zambia
9K	Kuwait
9L	Sierra Leone
9M	Malaysia
9N	Nepal
9Q	Zaire
9U	Burundi
9V	Singapore
9XR	Rwanda
9Y	Trinidad & Tobago
-	Belau (Palau)